THE
ADVERSITY
PARADOX

THE
ADVERSITY
PARADOX

An Unconventional Guide
to Achieving Uncommon
Business Success

J. BARRY GRISWELL
AND BOB JENNINGS

St. Martin's Press ♊ New York

www.stmartins.com

Library of Congress Cataloging-in-Publication Data

Griswell, J. Barry.
The adversity paradox : an unconventional guide to achieving uncommon business
success / J. Barry Griswell and Bob Jennings.
    p.   cm.
Includes bibliographical references.
ISBN-13: 978-0-312-38555-2
ISBN-10: 0-312-38555-2
1. Success in business.   I. Jennings, Bob, 1959–   II. Title.
HF5386.G777   2009
650.1—dc22   2008037580

First Edition: April 2009

10 9 8 7 6 5 4 3 2 1

This book is dedicated to all those
who have come from humble beginnings
and have overcome adversity and gone on
to make positive contributions to society;
to those who have experienced
midcareer setbacks and recovered;
and especially to those young people who
are struggling to overcome hardships.

CONTENTS

INTRODUCTION

My coauthor, Bob Jennings, and I believe that everyone aspiring to be successful in business should read this book—MBA students, entrepreneurs, managers, corporate leaders, those just entering the workforce, those with languishing careers. Anyone interested in learning the distinguishing characteristics of those who've been at the bottom and have risen to unimaginable levels of success will benefit from reading *The Adversity Paradox*. We make this bold claim not because we have the last word on attaining success, but because we've been moved, challenged, and inspired by what the people featured here have to teach, and we believe you will be, too.

The roots of this book actually started many years ago. I grew up in a very difficult environment. We were very poor, my family life was unstable, and had I continued on my original trajectory, I might have ended up in jail or even dead. But somehow, despite a terribly troubled start, I was able to achieve success both in business and in my personal life.

For a long time I didn't give much thought to what I now see was a fairly amazing turnaround. But when I moved into management positions and needed to recruit and retain high-quality team members, I began to think about the factors that contributed to the success of employees. I encountered people at every point of the success continuum, from those who proved to be outstanding to those who looked promising but ended as out-and-out failures. Why was it that the candidates with the flawless résumés—top grade point averages at the best schools, all the right internships, prestigious awards—sometimes proved to be our most disappointing hires? Conversely, why was it that candidates who didn't look so good on paper sometimes turned out to be invaluable team members and employees? Of course, there were exceptions on both sides, but after many successes and failures in the hiring process I began to suspect that there was one trait above all else that reliably predicted that a person would be successful. And it had been right there under my nose, reflected in my own personal story, all along: It was experience in overcoming adversity.

In my latter years of going down this learning curve, my good friend and coauthor Bob Jennings was doing a lot of international recruiting and hiring for his organization. Despite vast geographical and cultural differences, he found the very same thing I had: With few exceptions, if you compared two people with similar educational backgrounds and work experiences, those who'd demonstrated the ability to overcome adversity had a much better chance of succeeding down the road. We continually compared notes, each working to improve our own success trajectories but not thinking a great deal about what our conclusion meant beyond building our own first-class organizations.

Then in 2003 I was inducted into the Horatio Alger Association, an organization that recognizes individuals who have achieved success in spite of significant adversity. The role of adversity in the formation of business savvy and subsequent success suddenly rose to prominence as Bob and I learned the stories of these amazing folks. Soon enough, it seemed as if everywhere we turned we heard or read more stories of people who had overcome adversity and gone on to achieve success. Every story reinforced my earlier suspicion that an individual's overcoming adversity was the single most significant factor in predicting future success. So Bob and I decided to embark on a journey to find out if my hunch was true.

We conducted interviews and read books, Web sites, articles, and profiles, all the while continuing to gather anecdotal evidence. In the end we studied the lives of hundreds who'd overcome adversity, and some had stories so compelling that we went beyond quantitative research and sought them out for interviews. As suspected, we found the pearls of wisdom below the surface, not in the biographies or the history books. Many of these people exhibited great humility and used such terminology as "luck" and being "at the right place at the right time" to describe their paths to success. But underneath the veneer, each one had a definition of luck that had nothing to do with a fortuitous break or a chance connection, and they all related similar experiences of how overcoming adversity had played such a crucial role in their success trajectories that they now considered adversity their friend. Once we'd gathered all our data, we set out to determine the common characteristics present in these people and how they used the knowledge they'd gained in "befriending adversity" to build the business savvy that enabled their success. *The Adversity Paradox,* which we have written jointly unless otherwise indicated, is the result of the journey we took to find answers to our questions. We're honored to share the results with you.

Adversity is not an absolute requirement for building business savvy or for being successful. But it has provided an invaluable crucible of learning for the business leaders featured in *The Adversity Paradox,* and while you may not experience the extreme forms of adversity they did, it's inevitable that each and every one of us will encounter adversity at some point in our careers. We hope that you'll learn how to make adversity your friend and apply the lessons learned from overcoming it to positively impact your success trajectory. We hope you'll not only gain inspiration from these incredible paths to success but also identify concrete steps you can take to increase your own business savvy. We hope you'll be emboldened to take action or refocus your determination in your career path. We hope, too, you will pass on to others what you learn. But, above all, we hope you will take away a new-found understanding of yourself and the confidence you need to maximize your business savvy and attain outstanding success.

The Adversity Paradox's lessons are practical and inspirational, and you can apply them at any stage of your career. You can build a trajectory that will take you to previously unimagined levels of success. You can be one of those people who emerges from even the most humble of beginnings or the most devastating of setbacks to achieve the success you've always dreamed of. As these stories will show, no dream is ever impossible.

—J. Barry Griswell

THE
ADVERSITY
PARADOX

What Is Business Savvy, Anyway?

Main Entry: **business savvy**
Pronunciation: \\'biz-nəs 'sa-vē\\
Function: *noun*
1: proficiency in the realm of business; the unique ability to consistently meet and surpass one's business goals
Function: *adjective*
1: those who are proficient in business and consistently achieve outstanding success

Main Entry: **the adversity paradox**
Pronunciation: \\thə ad-'vər-sə-tē 'per-ə-.däks\\
Function: *noun*
1: the phenomenon of building outstanding success upon the lessons learned in overcoming serious difficulty or misfortune
var.: ***The Adversity Paradox***
Function: *proper noun*
1: a book that will help you learn how overcoming adversity may be the best preparation for business success you'll ever have

Business savvy is not something you're born with, nor is it something you inherit. But as we believe it is the key to business success, we start with the end in mind, defining what it is.

Everyone you'll meet in *The Adversity Paradox* possesses phenomenal business savvy, and the spark that first set it off was a firsthand encounter in overcoming some sort of adversity. But what exactly *is* business savvy? The above definitions spell it out, but more simply, you might call it "business sense" or "business instinct," and you might say that those who possess it are "business smart" or just plain "successful." But we like "business savvy" because it neatly describes both the people who possess it and the acquired competencies they gain by befriending adversity. So before we talk about the adversity paradox, we're going to devote some time to examining business savvy in detail. This discussion will be the foundation for all that follows: a close look at how a wide variety of people overcame adversity and achieved great success, and how the lessons they learned from their experiences can help you do the same.

So how much business savvy would you say you have? Enough to purchase an insolvent company with a dozen employees and grow it to a $100 million business, *and* pen some of the bestselling business books of all time? Enough to, despite having no business background whatsoever, start a business in your basement that goes on to become a household name, with sales of more than $700 million? Do you have enough business savvy to arrive in a new country with very little money, do whatever it takes to put yourself through school, and within a handful of years rise from an entry-level position to the top spot in the company? How about the kind of business savvy that takes you from an early life marked by poverty, a broken home, struggles with learning, and the lowest of expectations all the way to the executive suite? Or the kind of business savvy that enables you to carry an aviation company through the storm after 9/11, or the kind that makes it possible to pick yourself up after the sudden separation from a decades-long career and emerge with an even stronger and more fulfilling purpose? No matter what type of adversity life throws at you, do you have the wherewithal to resist giving up and to pursue your passion-driven goals all the way to their successful completion?

Maybe not yet, but this book will introduce you to those who've acquired the insight the adversity paradox has to teach: Working to overcome humble beginnings, lack of knowledge, major unexpected setbacks, or any manner of misfortune that life throws your way may be the greatest tool for building business savvy you'll ever possess. The business leaders you'll meet in *The Adversity Paradox* have overcome all manner of adversity and used their experiences to create the business savvy that enabled them to attain unmatched levels of success. In short, they've found a way to befriend adversity and put it to work for them. They've turned failure on its head and have built successful careers *and* personal lives upon the very experiences most people work assiduously to avoid.

Here's the thing about adversity: If you can make it your friend, you may find yourself in one of the most powerful and transformative situations that life has to offer. Of course we'd never advocate going out and seeking difficult circumstances in order to develop yourself or further your career, but the fact is setbacks are going to happen—certainly in the business world. An investment can go bad. An important employee or partner could desert you. A counted-on sale may go to your biggest competitor. An important deal could go upside down on you. But it's in how one deals with these unexpected misfortunes that separates those who fail from those who attain the top levels of success.

Perhaps it's a sad fact, but success absolutely does not provide the impetus for improvement that adversity does. Say you just sold a new client, won a promotion or a pay raise, or gave a presentation that drew rave reviews. What's the result? High fives around the office, a pat on the back at home, or a toast over dinner. Sure, you should enjoy the well-deserved accolades, but be wary: In the face of success we can become complacent. It's far too easy to become too satisfied with our current performance and get a little lax on improving.

In contrast, what happens after a failure or some personal heartache? Ideally we immediately analyze the situation to see what went wrong and we focus on what we could've done differently. No one likes to go through adversity, but faced with the right attitude, a difficult setback can be one of our most powerful catalysts for change. Adversity can provide the motivation and the determination to sharpen our skills and regain our focus, and that in turn has a direct positive impact on the creation of business savvy.

If there's one thing we'd like you to take away from this book, it's the certainty that you always have a choice. No matter how terrible the setback—and in this book you'll meet some people who overcame "impossible" situations—you can make the choice to lie back and let adversity consume you, or you can face the situation head-on and work to make adversity your friend. Befriending adversity means not shying from it, but learning from it. It means not letting it defeat you, but laboring to overcome it, and even better, using what you learn from the experience to improve yourself. Those who've been tested by the fires of adversity and have passed the test emerge stronger, smarter, and savvier.

Oddly enough, though the stories in this book are quite diverse, the attributes evinced by these business-savvy individuals are remarkably similar. That's because they've made certain core competencies—ones that consistently get superior results—part of their daily practice. Pause for a moment and think of the most successful business people you know. We'll bet they comprehend things quickly and are able to synthesize vast amounts of data and drill down to the salient points. They're naturally intuitive and can size up situations and people virtually on the spot through their ability to empathize with others' positions. They're resourceful and innovative in matters both practical and abstract, even visionary. They're knowledgeable and perceptive, and if they discover an information void, they act quickly to fill it. They act promptly but judiciously on information, and they exhibit wisdom and sound reasoning in matters large and small.

But for people with business savvy borne of adversity, there is so much more to the story. The business leaders who've benefited from the adversity paradox are the ones who use the diagnostic skill of introspection to conduct honest self-assessments so as to make trajectory adjustments whenever necessary. They're the employees with outstanding personal values—values they never check at the company door. They're the ones with a superior work character, who often arrive at the office before everyone else and leave later—and love it. For them a job is never just the five days standing in the way of the weekend or the means to an easy retirement. These folks have found a purpose they're passionate about and have found a way to take the work out of work. They're the employees who nurture a thirst for knowledge that keeps them constantly abreast of the ever-changing world of business.

Given such commendable core competencies and practices, it isn't surprising that those who've learned their lessons the hard way often go on to achieve enormous wealth as a result of their prodigious business savvy. Who comes to mind when you think of incredibly successful businesspeople? Richard Branson, Warren Buffett, Bill Gates, Wayne Huizenga, Oprah Winfrey? They're all good answers, and in fact every one of them has been listed in *Forbes*'s March 2008 issue on billionaires. Winfrey's experiences of adversity are the best known: A female minority from an underprivileged background, she has become one of the country's most successful and admired businesspeople, with assets now reaching $2.5 billion. Like Winfrey, you can bet that every one of these business-savvy individuals has encountered adversity, overcome it, and used what they learned to maximize their business savvy. Adversity doesn't defeat them but propels them to succeed.

Now, it's true that most of us will never achieve the level of success and fame that Oprah Winfrey and Warren Buffett have, but the good news about the adversity paradox is that anyone— yes, anyone—can learn how overcoming his or her own personal misfortunes can improve business savvy. This book is for the *rest of us*—the young worker with his foot on the bottom rung of the corporate ladder, the small business owner, the midlevel manager, or even the CEO who's interested in raising his overall performance.

So let's meet a man whose life is an example par excellence of the adversity paradox in action. Like yours, his may not be a household name, but the kind of success he's achieved, both in business and in his personal life, is something to which we all aspire. Like many in America, he was an immigrant with many strikes against him. But like a select few, he overcame the adversities life dealt him and built his success upon the very misfortunes that stop most in their tracks.

John Pappajohn

John Pappajohn was born in Greece and immigrated with his mother to the United States while he was still an infant. Mother and son settled in Mason City, Iowa, where Pappajohn's father had gone a year earlier to open a small neighborhood grocery store. Pappajohn's family spoke Greek exclusively at home, and as learning English proved to be difficult, his kindergarten teacher held him back a year so he could catch up with his peers. What he did not find difficult was work. At the age of eight he was a rag merchant and a junk collector. He scavenged for rags, brass, copper, and lead and sold scrap to the local junk dealer.

When he was a little older, he joined his father in working at the grocery store. Then when he was sixteen, tragedy struck: His father died, leaving Pappajohn to manage the store. He was now the head of the household, left to support two younger brothers and a mother who spoke no English. His father's death and the sudden responsibility that fell to Pappajohn were difficult, to say the least, but the experience he gained by living through those adversities created a firm basis for the development of the business savvy that would later make him so successful. "You become successful by solving your problems and overcoming adversity," he said. "The grocery store was hard work, but it was a wonderful learning experience. It also kept our family afloat. We had one financial pot and all the earnings from the store went to support the family."

Money was tight, but the Pappajohns believed wholeheartedly in the power of education, so John and his brothers took turns putting each other through college. After graduating with a degree in business administration, he again worked at the family grocery store, but also went into insurance. Eventually he relocated to Des Moines and became the original organizer of Guardsman Insurance. "My experience at the grocery store assisted me greatly in the organization of Guardsman," Pappajohn said. "I knew about customer service, delivering a superior product, sticking with it through tough times, and as I was the oldest of three boys in a family without a father, I learned very quickly that you do what you have to do. I'd also gained outstanding business judgment, which is an asset in running any business."

While Pappajohn found success in insurance, he didn't develop a true passion for it. So he researched new opportunities, and for the first time read about venture capital. "It looked like the perfect opportunity for me," he said. "So I made a commitment to myself, to my family, and to my friends that I was going to be a venture capitalist and from that point forward, I could not back down." In 1969 he founded Equity Dynamics, a venture capital firm.

Pappajohn has been enormously successful in venture capitalism, and he is now committed to helping others find the same kind of success. The John and Mary Pappajohn Entrepreneurial Centers have helped create and launch more than a thousand new companies. "I'm now in the unusual position that I can finance big dreams for people with big ideas," he said. "That's what it's all about—helping other people succeed."

Pappajohn's early experiences with adversity—the death of

his father, the onset of serious family and work responsibilities at a young age, limited financial resources—have remained with him throughout his adult life and career. But while some would find even one of these challenges sufficient reason to give up or to lower their goals, Pappajohn credits these very things as crucial ingredients in his success. At the grocery store he learned all aspects of the business and how to make decisions on his own. He gained a certain level of maturity much earlier than most. He also learned that he wanted to go into business for himself, which was the foundational step in what has proved to be an extraordinary career. Today, he goes to great lengths to make educational and business opportunities available to those who need assistance. His career and his life illustrate the adversity paradox in action.

Let's now take a closer look at his business savvy in action. We'd like to show you how Pappajohn's early experiences with adversity played out in his career many years later, and how what he learned by overcoming adversity contributed directly to his business savvy.

Pappajohn the Venture Capitalist

Pappajohn describes his job as "financing, advising, raising capital, and market consulting." He has served as a director of more than forty public companies and has been involved in more than fifty public financings. "I'm often seen as a company doctor," he said. Unlike a doctor, he makes an initial financial investment, stays actively involved with his patients through adolescence, and gets paid only if his patients turn into superstars. In short, he supplies business savvy to small start-up companies, helps grow them, and not only sees entrepreneurs' dreams realized but lots of millionaires made in the process. And, of course, he makes a buck or two for himself. After years of successful ventures, Pappajohn is a very wealthy man, and one of the wonderful things about him is that he enjoys giving money away even more than he enjoys making it.

At any one time he could be personally invested in and working closely with as many as twenty companies—a roster of pertinent information he keeps track of with handwritten notes he carries in his pocket. He's always keeping score, and over the thirty-eight years Equity Dynamics has been in business it has averaged a 50 percent annual return. At the time we interviewed Pappajohn, he had a sixteen-year track record in excess of 100 percent. Many of his ventures have been in the health-care industry and involve the supply of goods, services, and new technologies. It's an industry he has come to understand extremely well. Because of his vast institutional knowledge and experience, his estimation of what he can help grow and prosper and what he cannot assist is spot-on. Given his industry reputation, he's often approached with deals, and looks at more than a hundred opportunities a year. He selects only those that meet his investment criteria.

We knew John Pappajohn personally and by reputation, and we knew of his prodigious business savvy and that his life exemplified the adversity paradox in action. But we wanted to gain an even better understanding of how he actually applies his hard-earned business savvy and how he makes a living doing so. So we asked one of his former presidents to take us through an insider's view of how Pappajohn accomplishes a deal. Doug Stickney is the cofounder and former CEO of one of Pappajohn's ventures turned superstar, Quantum Health Resources Inc. Pappajohn and Stickney first became acquainted in 1985 when

Stickney was employed at his father's start-up business, Western Medical Specialties (WMS). Between its start in 1979 and 1983 the company had grown profitably to $1 million in sales. In late 1983 Stickney began working for his father, and by 1985 the business grew to $10 million in sales but needed money and expertise in order to maintain its rapid growth. To find both, Stickney's father turned to John Pappajohn.

Pappajohn agreed to help in exchange for the opportunity to buy a stake in the company, up to 10 percent. Pappajohn envisioned easily growing the business to a point where they could go public. Then two weeks after striking the deal, a large healthcare services company came knocking on the door with a $10 million offer to buy WMS outright. With Pappajohn's blessing, Stickney's dad accepted the offer. This would have been a quick windfall for Pappajohn, but he refused his 10 percent stake, saying that he had done nothing to deserve the money. It was immediately obvious to both father and son that Pappajohn was a man of integrity, a man who would be a respectful and honorable partner in business.

Doug Stickney continued to work for WMS. After another ownership change he decided to go out on his own. He wanted to create a network of pharmacies around the country that would cater specifically to unique home health markets. Stickney was thirty-two at the time, had some industry experience, and was well educated, with a bachelor's degree from Davidson College and a master's in biostatistics from UCLA. What he lacked was the money to get the business off the ground. Remembering the positive experience his father had had with Pappajohn and the impression of confidence and trust Pappajohn had engendered, Stickney gave him a call. "I knew I had the right guy in Doug Stickney," Pappajohn later said, smiling. "He had grown his dad out of business."

Pappajohn also had invaluable insight for Stickney. Having been involved in a number of health-care start-ups he knew "the space," as he calls it, very well, and with health-care costs going through the roof, he recognized a future of less in-patient care and more in-home care. He could also see that the business infrastructure needed to service in-home health care had yet to be created, and like many of his ventures this was an opportunity to be one of the first providers into the space. With many years of business experience, Pappajohn knew exactly what needed to be accomplished and believed that they could help build a successful public health-care company.

Within three weeks of their first phone conversation, Pappajohn wired Stickney $200,000, and in 1988 Quantum Health Resources Inc. was founded. The premise of the business was to set up pharmacies that, unlike the traditional street-corner Walgreens, had a focus of cost-effective delivery of high-quality therapies and services to individuals affected by chronic conditions such as hemophilia, α_1 antitrypsin deficiency, HIV/AIDS, autoimmune disorders, growth hormone deficiencies, cystic fibrosis, primary pulmonary hypertension, and Lou Gehrig's disease. Stickney would serve as president and CEO while Pappajohn would mentor and play a role as a key board member.

One of the first things he recommended to Stickney was that all votes by the board needed to be unanimous—there could never be questionable direction for the young company. "And Pappajohn made sure of that," Stickney said. "He had incredible listening skills. He'd collect all the information he could before taking a position, and then he had the ability to counsel other board members, some more experienced than he in various areas, and gain the unanimous votes necessary to act."

Stickney, along with three other executives he'd brought in as cofounders, worked for the first six months strictly for sweat equity. They invested all they had, $180,000, but things moved quickly. By the end of 1988 they had a dozen paid employees, and by early 1989 Stickney and Pappajohn decided to visit Wall Street to get a feel for the viability of and investor interest in eventually taking the company public. Once again Pappajohn acted as an invaluable mentor. It was Stickney's first foray on Wall Street, while Pappajohn had a reputation for pounding the pavement in New York City, scheduling as many investor calls as could be fitted into a day (and then some) and then running from meeting to meeting at a feverish pace. Their first day Pappajohn scheduled five presentations in which Stickney did the talking and Pappajohn remained silent. In hindsight, Stickney realized that these were what Pappajohn would deem second-tier prospects: Pappajohn was preparing Stickney for the big leagues.

Between 1988 and 1991 Quantum grew from zero to $100 million in sales and expanded to seven pharmacies. In those first three years the business would require $10 million of added investment to cover start-up losses and provide working capital, primarily for inventory. There were three rounds of fund-raising and with each new round the company needed to negotiate a new valuation, which Stickney agonized over continually. The shares of stock given to new investors diluted the founders' and initial investors' ownership in the company. Valuing stock in each new issue is a difficult task, as the owners are selling what they believe is opportunity, as opposed to historical earnings. If they value the stock too low, they hurt themselves, while valuing too high risks unhappy investors. Stickney turned to Pappajohn for advice. "Always remember," Pappajohn said, "pigs get fat and hogs get slaughtered." The reasonable valuations Stickney subsequently agreed to not only got investors in, but each and every investor returned for every round. By negotiating reasonable valuations, Stickney ensured no investors were disappointed with the outcome and results, and in the end all who made initial investments or invested with sweat equity—who worked for stock rather than a paycheck—were very well rewarded.

Stickney, Pappajohn, and the board decided to take Quantum public in April 1991. Then, just a few months before the offering, an employee approached Stickney with a $50,000 tax problem and a request for a loan. The employee was Stickney's brother. Faced with the touchy dilemma, Stickney again sought advice from Pappajohn. His response was stern but sound: "Every decision you make you must imagine that it will be public and will be in our prospectus for our public stock offering," he said. "Now, what do you think potential investors will think when they read you loaned a family member money?" Then Pappajohn sought out Stickney's brother and set up a meeting. Pappajohn personally provided him a loan, which was kept off of the company's balance sheet and was later repaid.

The public offering was a resounding success, and the three-year-old Quantum Health Resources achieved a valuation of $150 million. It operated for five years as a public company before being acquired. At its peak, Quantum had a market valuation of more than $800 million and 1,500 employees. Pappajohn's $200,000 investment had a value of more than $40 million and at the same time created over a dozen employee millionaires, including Stickney. Stickney states today, "Everyone involved knew Pappajohn made a big hit on the deal, and we couldn't have been any happier for him."

The Business-Savvy Profile

An examination of John Pappajohn's road to success reveals an impressive roster of business-savvy competencies—as will examinations of all the people you'll meet later in this book. Though Pappajohn is an entrepreneur, these business-savvy competencies can be found in any profession, including the one you're in. Let's take a look at them, and as you read, ask yourself if you possess them and, if so, how proficient you are in each area. Plenty of people are good, but the business savvy are great— *consistently* great.

Systems and Linear Thinking

One reason John Pappajohn has done so well is that he is able to see and understand thoroughly his area of business as a whole. For Pappajohn this is the health-care industry, but clearly the ability to discern and understand the big picture is essential for whatever area of business you're in. In Pappajohn's case, he reads widely and talks to people constantly, so he knows what direction the industry is going and why, any trends or new technologies that may affect the market, and any voids that may be present, which allows him to anticipate emerging needs ahead of others. He also keeps an eye on the state of the economy, inflation, the competition, and consumer demand, just as anyone wishing to do well in business must. In the 1980s he realized that there would be a growing demand for home health care to combat rising medical costs, and he was able to position himself to fill that need. More recently, he perceived a pressing need for noninvasive methods to diagnose cancer, and he invested in companies designing these devices. At the same time, Pappajohn is always on the lookout for small companies that have the ability to fill the needs he has identified. Simply stated, he has gained a comprehensive view of the health-care industry that allows him to see where all the pieces of the puzzle may fit.

The kind of global thinking we're talking about is known as *systems thinking*. In his seminal book, *The Fifth Discipline*, Peter Senge describes systems thinking as the "discipline for seeing the wholes." It's "a framework," he writes, "for seeing interrelationships rather than things, for seeing patterns of change rather than static snapshots."

But it doesn't stop there for the truly business savvy. Business-savvy professionals need to see and understand not only the sum of all the parts, but also the parts themselves. The kind of thinking required to do this is the opposite of systems thinking, or *linear thinking*. As its name implies, linear thinking involves following a straight path. Much of the work done in any business is execution and involves linear thinking. It's a mind-set of closing the world out so as to concentrate exclusively on the execution of the task at hand in order to complete it as quickly and efficiently as possible. The best practice in business has always been to try to define jobs and processes in a linear arrangement in order to lower the cost of production of goods or services. A variety of means have been used for developing the best linear arrangements, including theory of constraints, Six Sigma, lean manufacturing, and business process management.

When Pappajohn got involved with Quantum, the business was

at its most rudimentary stage: There were four founders, no pay-roll, and, at best, the beginnings of a business plan. There were countless individual steps involved in taking it from nothing to a $40 million success—incorporation, cash flow, filling key positions, marketing plans, site selections, contracting, structuring and restructuring, investors, company boards, growing from a four-person team to one of 1,500. The list goes on and on. At every step and with every detail, he was involved in growing the business, either hands-on or in a coaching role. If there was a lack of attention to pertinent details along the way, the fledgling company could have sputtered and died.

Business-savvy people not only need to be adept at both systems and linear thinking, but also must have a feel for when to employ systems thinking and when to go linear to get results. The business savvy can bounce back and forth between the two mind-sets quickly and easily. When they're in the linear mind-set and they run into obstacles or setbacks, they're able to step back, put on the systems thinking hat, and rethink the system. After the big picture has been adequately reassessed and a new plan or path of action determined, their linear thinking comes immediately into play to get results, quickly and efficiently.

Continuous Thinking

It's often said that business leaders like Pappajohn are vision-ary, and while we wouldn't hesitate to describe him as such, there are very good explanations as to why business-savvy people such as Pappajohn can "see into the future." We've described one reason already: Pappajohn's systems thinking ability enables him to see the health-care industry as a whole, which allows him to anticipate needs in the market before anyone else does. But yet another explanation lies in another type of thinking the business savvy have mastered: *continuous thinking*.

On one level continuous thinking is just what its name implies. The business savvy's minds never turn off. They're constantly running what-if scenarios in their heads and assessing the general risks and rewards for potential outcomes. The practice of continuous thinking can often fuel audacious dreams and goals: If the mind is constantly churning, inspiration is more likely to strike. If Pappajohn and his team realize their vision with noninvasive cancer diagnostic devices, for example, it will do no less than revolutionize the health-care industry and alleviate a great deal of human suffering.

On another level, some would say that continuous thinking enables the business savvy to see around corners or predict the future. But the fact is, they don't always get it right—it just *looks* as if they did, as they are constantly formulating plans and making adjustments. "Every new venture has its ups and downs," Pappajohn said, "and literally not a single one of my ventures has ever come through without a change in plans along the way." Because his mind is constantly active, he can anticipate problems just as well as he can anticipate successes. Thus, he's formulated solutions well in advance, the only way to be proactive.

Synthesizing

With such a profusion of information, the business savvy need a superior ability to sort and prioritize data, especially in today's environment of information overload. Information comes at us faster than ever before, and it's available twenty-four hours a day. Plus, it arrives in greater quantities, and in many cases in ways we can't control: Between e-mail and text messaging, it's not at all uncommon for even the average person to receive between fifty and one hundred messages per day. Messaging alone can easily bog people down in a morass of data. With so much information cluttering the brain, we can easily turn into nothing more than data collectors. Thus an ability to sift, sort, prioritize, store, discard, and stitch together information sets the business savvy apart from others.

Synthesizing is exactly this process. It is the process of turning the data we receive into salient information. In the February 2006 issue of the *Harvard Business Review,* Harvard professor Howard Gardner writes about *The Synthesizing Leader.* Gardner states, "The ability to decide which data to heed, which to ignore, and how to organize and communicate information will be among the most important traits of business executives in this century." He goes on to reference the Nobel Prize–winning physicist Murray Gell-Mann, who thinks that the most valued personal trait of the twenty-first century will be a facility for synthesizing information.

Synthesizing is a necessary complement to continuous thinking, and even to systems thinking, both of which can end up overwhelming a person with data. The business savvy can easily discern the difference between data—what amounts to useless detail—and information that is vital to decision making. Many individuals drown in data, whereas the business savvy rise above the tides. They continually search and sift for good information to make sound decisions.

With the mountain of data that pummels Pappajohn every day from each company he works with (business plans, monthly financials, board reports, memos, e-mails, and phone calls are only the tip of the iceberg), plus the more than one hundred proposals he's given each year for potential investments, plus the inestimable intricacies of staying apprised of so many ventures at once, not to mention the overall health of the market, he simply could not manage, much less excel as he does, without being a master synthesizer. Ironically, Pappajohn uses a simple, even old-fashioned method to stay on top of the surfeit of information concerning his current business concerns: He keeps a handwritten list and carries it in his pocket.

Knowing What You Don't Know

The flip side to staying always on top of new information is knowing what you don't know. It's not as mysterious as it sounds. It's a matter of being aware of where your information voids are, of knowing where your area of expertise stops, and, in some cases, where another person's begins. It's also a matter of not acting until you obtain all the information necessary to make a sound decision. Some may accuse the business savvy of procrastination from time to time, but knowing that making decisions without an adequate information base can be detrimental to them and their businesses, they do not act until they're sufficiently informed.

What sets the business savvy apart from those who are merely aware of the voids in their knowledge base is how they deal with these gaps. The business savvy research and learn until the information void is filled, or, in cases of highly specialized knowledge, they delegate a task to a qualified individual or hire a person with the kind of human capital they need. In every situation, they are known for their penetrating questions. They're able to drill down until they've reached the root cause of a problem or uncovered the seeds of opportunity. This is how they make some of the most difficult things look intuitive.

Those who work with Pappajohn know of his ability to drill down with questions. He doesn't make a move until he's thoroughly researched the market, the business plan, the people involved with executing the plan, and the new business's chances of success. No one is surprised when Pappajohn turns down a business opportunity when even a small glitch with people, places, or timing shows up. But many are surprised that, coming from a man who goes out of his way to stay fully informed, one of the very reasons he turns down an opportunity amounts to knowing what he doesn't know. "There were certainly times when a deal sounded attractive and even quite lucrative that I declined to get involved," he said, "because I did not know the space like I knew I needed to." Those who are savvy-challenged would not act with such prudence. They would plunge in headlong despite not being adequately prepared.

Communication

Peter Senge identifies two types of communication within an organization—*discussion* and *dialogue*. He states, "In discussion, different views are presented and defended. In dialogue, different views are presented as a means toward discovering a new view. . . . Dialogues are diverging; they do not seek agreement but a richer grasp of complex issues."

The foundation for excellent communication of any type is excellent listening. Doug Stickney explicitly pointed out Pappajohn's skills at listening, but Pappajohn's ability to gain a unanimous vote from board members alone demonstrates both his listening and his communication abilities. Certainly there is dialogue among members, but if Pappajohn is convinced of the rightness of a certain position, he can and will use discussion to explain and endorse his opinion. That he gains that unanimous vote every time attests to his superior communication abilities.

The business savvy have a constant awareness of the uses of dialogue and discussion. They intuitively know when it's important to collect information and ideas. They know when unwavering direction and conviction are required, and they deliver marching orders. They know when and how to deliver the "rubber hits the road" or the "pedal to the metal" message.

Empathy

The business savvy have excellent intuition. This is because they know their area of business so thoroughly and are prepared to the extreme. It is also because in communicating and dealing with others, they have a superior ability to gain *empathy*. Empathy is the ability to understand intuitively the thoughts and feelings of other people, to "put yourself in their shoes." This enables the business savvy to have a good understanding of what others are thinking and feeling, which allows them to stay consistently a step or two ahead of the game.

When it came time to determine valuations for Quantum in its early days, Pappajohn in essence advised Stickney to think like an investor, to step into potential investors' shoes and determine what would draw them in and what would dissuade them. As we've seen, an inflated valuation would certainly have dissuaded them, so Stickney set a reasonable valuation, and not only did he find investors, every single investor returned, and everyone involved made money. Then, when Stickney ran up against the situation with his brother and turned to Pappajohn for advice, Pappajohn was able to put himself in the shoes of both Stickney and Quantum's potential investors. He felt for Stickney and his brother, but thinking like an investor, he also knew that a personal loan could not be funded by the company. In the end his empathic abilities allowed him to find a good solution for everyone.

Based upon Pappajohn's amazing success record, it's clear that he can walk in the shoes of employees, stockholders, potential investors, board members, and the customers of the companies in which he has invested. There is no better means for devising ways to keep employees happy and stockholders content or get a meeting of the minds among board members than being able to see the thoughts, feelings, desires, and objectives of others.

The Adversity Paradox

Especially if you're smack in the middle of adversity, perhaps it seems like a stretch, a leap of faith, to believe that overcoming difficulties will enable you to develop the type of business savvy that facilitates the kind of success Pappajohn has had. Well, it isn't! In fact, it shouldn't be hard to believe at all. If you can do with adversity the extraordinary things Pappajohn has done—if you can accept it, determine not to let it stop you, overcome it, and in fact use everything overcoming adversity taught you to your advantage—you can *expect* extraordinary results. The stories in this book are quite diverse, but everyone you'll meet here went through a similar process of experiencing adversity, overcoming it, and learning from their struggles—their *victorious* struggles.

Like it or not, adversity will find its way into every life. Some of you may be struggling with adversity right now, and some of you will be facing adversity down the road. But what if right now, as a first step, you begin to think of adversity in a different light? What if you think of adversity as an opportunity to make positive adjustments to your trajectory and to acquire the kind of business savvy you can't get through school, seminars, training programs, or even doing your job day to day? These "trajectory adjustments" are going to be part of your future. Let's make sure every adjustment leads upward.

The Adversity Paradox Takeaways:
How You Can Recognize Business Savvy

- Let's review the core competencies of the business savvy demonstrated by John Pappajohn, and then you can take your own business-savvy inventory:

  1. Systems thinking: seeing and understanding the big picture
  2. Linear thinking: seeing and understanding each discrete part of the big picture, and being able to close in on specific tasks and execute them
  3. Continuous thinking: having "visionary" skills, the ability to anticipate problems and opportunities, be prepared for them, and react quickly
  4. Synthesizing: the practice of sorting and prioritizing salient information from data
  5. Awareness of information gaps and voids: being constantly aware of where your information voids lie and

responding appropriately by learning more, turning to others for help, or both

6. Communication: the ability to communicate with either dialogue or discussion

7. Empathy: the ability to discern and identify with what others are thinking and feeling

2

The Individual Human Capital of the Business Savvy

Individual Human Capital

In the broadest sense, capital may be understood as wealth devoted to the production of additional wealth. That "wealth" could be anything from money to a house or condo, from a stock portfolio to a factory. Capital consists of assets capable of producing income or other useful outputs over a period of time. Similarly, *individual human capital* (HC) is an individual's portfolio of assets in which he or she has invested that can produce future positive outputs. Gary S. Becker, university professor of economics and sociology at the University of Chicago and 1992 Nobel Prize winner in economics, is the foremost expert on human capital. He states, "Economists regard expenditures on education, training, medical care, and so on as investments in human capital. They are called human capital because people cannot be separated from their knowledge, skills, health, or values in the way they can be separated from their financial and physical assets."

As we've seen from our own business experiences, individual human capital development is quickly becoming the most important organizational improvement strategy as companies compete in an era of globalization. Consider the fact that labor in China can be bought for fifty cents per hour and in India for twenty-eight cents. We believe that most businesses do care about their employees and are largely averse to the prospect of having to move their jobs overseas just to survive. To beat the outsourcing trend, forward-thinking employers are eager to help their employees develop the skills they need to be the best in their fields and improve their organizations' competitive positions. Human capital development is paramount in this endeavor.

Education, experience garnered on the job, specialized training, and self-improvement workshops are all excellent sources for human capital development. In this book we're specifically interested in how business-savvy leaders took the knowledge they gained from overcoming adversity and used it to develop their individual human capital and the subsequent business savvy that made them. Our research reveals that the business leaders who had benefited from the adversity paradox tended to build their success upon the same five components: *introspection, values behavior, work character, purpose and passion,* and *thirst for knowledge.* Together, we call this "the business-savvy framework." We'll be focusing on each of these components individually in later chapters, but for now we'd like to take you through one of our own experiences with the adversity paradox.

The Griswell Profile:
More Difficult Than It Looks

J. Barry Griswell is not only my coauthor but also my best friend, and he's one of the savviest business people around. It was his story of really tough beginnings and later flourishing as a result of the skills and knowledge he gained from overcoming adversity that first inspired us to write this book. Barry has successfully put all the components of the business-savvy framework together and built a rags-to-riches kind of success.

Like a lot of the overachievers we talked to in order to write this book, Barry displays tremendous humility. His humility, coupled with a natural reticence regarding the negative aspects of his past, made getting the real story a bit difficult. Barry was thoroughly cooperative, of course, but a couple of short anecdotes will show you what I mean. We've been close friends for seventeen years. We've played countless tennis matches together. Our families have vacationed together. Our spouses are very close. We even live on the same street. It's the type of relationship in which we care about each other's kids as much as we care for our own. Even so, when Barry was inducted into the Horatio Alger Association and a brief bio was given, I learned some things about him I'd never known. As you'll see, his is a story of really tough beginnings—a struggle with poverty and run-ins with the law. I was stunned to learn that both his dad and his stepfather had struggled with alcoholism and ultimately died prematurely as a result of their addictions.

There was much more to the man, much that he kept quiet,

and given his behavior on the tennis court, I should have known. One summer we entered a competitive tennis tournament together, and during a couple of doubles matches Barry slowed to almost a crawl. Our opponents smelled blood and continually pounded the ball at him mercilessly. Somehow we found a way to win, but after repeated matches in which Barry quickly tired and grew pale, it was clear that something wasn't right. He never said a word, and even when I asked he would not comment. He just wanted to get back on the court. He's a big guy at six nine, and I guess I just assumed he ran out of gas.

Then one week he disappeared for a couple of days. My wife and I received a call from his wife and learned that Barry was recovering from what he called "elective open-heart surgery" to correct a heart arrhythmia. He knew of the issue when we were in those tennis matches—his heart would go out of rhythm, beating at two hundred beats per minute when it should have been half that. Still, he offered no excuses, and he wouldn't quit. Soon enough, more stories came to light, like his sometimes having to leave the office during lunch to drop by the local hospital and have his heart shocked back into rhythm.

I'd always had the feeling he didn't appreciate people feeling sorry for him—which is fairly rare, as even the toughest of people seem to welcome some sympathy. In fact, if I want to get under his skin, as good friends can do, all I have to say is, "I feel sorry for you." But it was only in interviewing Barry for this book that I realized exactly where that attitude came from. What started out to be merely another profile in the book, a way to illustrate the key components of the business-savvy framework, became a real eye-opener for me.

My Coauthor's Story

John Barry Griswell was born and raised in Atlanta, Georgia. His mom, June Griswell, dropped out of high school at age sixteen when she eloped with his dad, J.B., who was then twenty-four. His mother tried to keep her marriage a secret but wasn't able to and was forced to drop out of school. His dad, a factory worker for a short time and used-car salesman, never attended high school. Barry described his father as "a restless sort," a man who played in a band, dabbled in business, and enjoyed drinking. "My father was a bit of an entrepreneur and a free spirit," Barry said. "He always wanted to be in business for himself and he opened several used-car lots over the years but lacked the ability and education to achieve any success. At one point he sold all our furniture to start a used-car lot. To replace the furniture he rented more, but it took only a couple of months before rental payments surpassed the proceeds from the furniture sale. It seemed like he focused on get-rich-quick schemes rather than career building. He ended up following his family tradition of operating an upholstery business."

As the years passed, Barry's father grew increasingly dependent upon alcohol. "When he wasn't drinking," Barry said, "he was a wonderful person and was very kind." But when he drank too much, he became obsessively jealous toward Barry's mom, and then grew belligerent and abusive. One incident in particular stands out in Barry's mind; he was five years old when the scene happened. "One night my older brother and I were awakened by the sounds of a fight. My dad was drunk and throwing things at our mother, anything he could get his hands on—pots, pans, even hamburger meat and eggs. Somehow in the chaos Mother managed to get to a phone. She called her father, and she and my brother and I ran for it. We waited in the parking lot for my grandfather to pick us up and take us to his house."

June divorced J.B. while Barry was still a small child, but, as often happens, she went back to her abuser, and they remarried. Her own parents had been through a messy, painful divorce, and she swore she'd never put her children through such an experience. She tried very hard to make the marriage work, but in the end the problems were insurmountable. June and J.B. divorced a second and final time, all before Barry was six years old. Barry recently told me that the last straw for his mother was when his father came home drunk and literally kicked her out of bed and into the hall.

The abuse didn't stop after the divorce. June got a job at a trucking company as a receptionist and switchboard operator, and at her first Christmas party her now ex-husband showed up drunk and disrupted the party by throwing food. She was terrified that she would lose her job.

The income was especially needed because Barry's father didn't pay child support regularly and often got months behind. At various times, when June attempted to have him put in jail, Barry and his brother would persuade her not to. This situation put financial strains on the family for years. To make ends meet, June had to work two jobs. In addition to her job as switchboard operator, where she worked forty hours a week, she worked as a receptionist at an emergency clinic from six P.M. to midnight. "She would work her day job, come home and cook dinner for my older brother and me, and then head off to her night job," Barry recalled. "In those early years my mom was my only role model. She demonstrated not only a tremendous work ethic but what was expected of you when you were employed. She went to work no matter what, even if she was sick." She remained at her main job for the next thirty years and worked at a variety of part-time jobs during that time.

Despite the two jobs, Barry's mom found it difficult to support the family. Barry's grandmother tried to help out, and for many years the family of four lived in small one- or two-bedroom apartments. When they fell behind on the rent, they moved to another apartment complex under a different name. For years, they engaged in a round-robin style of living, making stops among three different apartment complexes in a continual quest to stay ahead of rent payments. By the time Barry became a teenager, he and his family had moved thirteen times. "All that moving left me a little shell-shocked," Barry admitted. "I was in a new school every six to nine months, and never had a chance to make stable friendships. I ended up being a very shy kid."

Fortunately, Barry's home life had been stable for the first three or four years of his life. "I now see that period of stability as a gift," Barry said. "I at least had a foundation of normalcy that I could draw upon—my father was working, my mother was home to take care of us, and we stayed in one place. And, even after all the troubles began, I still had a loving mother, a grandmother who was there for us, and an older brother who helped look after me."

To help make ends meet, Barry began working at an early age. He and his brother had a paper route, and he sacked groceries at a market that was in the middle of an all-black neighborhood. "I was the only white person working there and I delivered groceries in the area around the store," Barry said. "In those days racial tensions were still very high in the South, and it was difficult for anyone to understand diversity. I think this experience was key to my learning to appreciate our differences at a young age." In high school, he worked as a lifeguard at a city public pool and for the trucking company where his mother was employed. He loaded trucks at night and on weekends, making $3 an hour, which at the time was good money. That job allowed him to buy a car and take care of his own expenses throughout high school, college, and graduate school. "My jobs as a kid—a paper route, sacking groceries, lifeguarding at an inner-city pool, spending a summer on a garbage truck and then loading trucks at night and on weekends," Barry said, "were all about just trying to satisfy some very basic needs, some financial security as much as anything. We were poor and there just wasn't money left over to do anything. Today, I feel so fortunate to have worked hard as a kid. Not for the money I made, but for the physical work ethic I developed."

Despite his work responsibilities and involvement in sports, Barry found time to get in trouble. He and his brother were largely left on their own, with little parental instruction. They saw their father only on weekends, and sometimes not even then, and June was usually at work. Barry ended up having to make decisions about what to do and when to do it at an age when many kids make few, if any, decisions. He may have gained a certain measure of maturity from this, but all the idle time and the lack of supervision mostly worked against him. At one point he hooked up with some kids who killed time by vandalizing cars. "I got caught my very first time," Barry said, with a laugh. "That should've told me something." Because the crime happened on a Friday, Barry spent all weekend in youth detention, the equivalent of jail for juveniles. His mother picked him up on a Monday morning, and the memory of how angry and disappointed she was has never left him. She looked at his detention paper with disgust. "That piece of paper in your hand is going to go right on the mantel," she said, "right alongside your basketball trophies. That'll be a reminder to you!"

"It really should have been," Barry said, "but I was hard-headed and too easily swayed by what the crowd was doing, and it would be years before I'd get straightened out."

When a new adult figure did arrive in Barry's life, he wasn't a good influence. Barry's mother became acquainted with a man who was a friend of her sister. This man was later charged as an accomplice to a crime and served time in a county jail. When her sister and brother-in-law went to visit him, June went along. They began writing each other, and soon enough she was visiting him every Sunday afternoon, taking eleven-year-old Barry with her. The couple fell in love, and when Barry was twelve, his soon-to-be stepfather was released and married his mother. When Barry was fifteen, and his mother forty, his second brother was born.

The new family had some good times in the early years, especially as his stepfather supported Barry in athletics, but Barry's stepfather, like his father, also had trouble handling alcohol. He worked as a mechanic, but after a while his drinking binges prevented him from keeping steady work. "He would sometimes stay drunk for days," Barry said. "We had a house by then, but we lost it because of his drinking and ended up back at another apartment complex." Not surprisingly, Barry and his older brother each butted heads with their stepfather from time to time.

One of their worst fights occurred when Barry was seventeen. Barry came home late one Friday night to find his stepfather pushing his mom around. Barry went after his stepfather and the two men fought. During the struggle, Barry grabbed a

.22-caliber rifle his father had given him. But somehow, in a way he still can't explain, his right index finger got caught in the loading chamber and was badly cut—an amazingly fortuitous occurrence that prevented his or his stepfather's death. He still carries a scar from that fight, a constant reminder of a narrowly avoided disaster.

The marriage between his mother and stepfather ended in divorce after five years. Barry's childhood and adolescence were intensely troubled years, but at least one good emerged: What he witnessed hurt badly enough that he was motivated to seek and make a better life for himself and his family.

There were also, he is quick to point out, plenty of positive things to keep him from going off the deep end entirely. Church was a positive influence that would become much more important later on, and despite all the tumult in his house, there was, as he put it, "no lack of love. My mother and grandmother were always very loving and caring individuals." He was also extremely fortunate to become involved in the Atlanta Boys Club, where he boxed and played basketball. By the time he was in the eighth grade, he was six four and well on his way to his adult height of six nine. He became a star basketball player for his high school team and was the talk of the town. The success enabled him to start envisioning a future for himself beyond high school. As for so many others, athletics became a valuable alternative for Barry's spare time and energy. "It was a wonderful outlet for me in the afternoon after school," he said, "and it became a very important part of my life." He credits the Boys Club with keeping him off the streets and out of a lot worse trouble.

And he credits his mother with stressing the value of education. "My mother wanted my brother and me to have a better life, so she pushed hard for us to do well in school," Barry said. "She knew how important education was and that it could be a means to a better life." But learning proved to be a difficult obstacle. "I was neither a naturally gifted nor motivated student, and learning was a struggle," he said. "I struggled with reading, and I had to attend summer school to keep up with my peers."

Perhaps one of the greatest influences on Barry was his childhood sweetheart—now his wife of almost forty years—and her family. "Michele and I met in the eighth grade and started dating at age sixteen after taking a French class together," Barry recalled. There was no question that she and her father, a Baptist minister, were key to keeping Barry on track through college and graduate school and getting him off to a good start in business. "My wife's father quickly became a mentor to me," he said. "Every time I had a major decision to make, I would confide in Bill. He would never make the decision for me but would always help me think through it. He was the father I didn't have, and I am eternally grateful to him."

Barry persevered, and eventually these positive influences—faith, basketball, education, and a good mentor—came together in a way he couldn't have foreseen: He earned a basketball scholarship to Berry College, a private college in northern Georgia, becoming the second member of his family to graduate from high school and the first to attend college. No stranger to work by now, he worked twenty hours a week in the school bookstore to supplement his scholarship. Given Barry's success on the basketball court and the high regard he had for coaches, without whom he says he would've been lost as a child, he planned either to play professional basketball or, if that didn't happen, be a teacher and coach.

During his first couple of years at college he began second-guessing the future he'd planned on. Basketball was no longer as fun and exciting as it had once been. "While I was pursuing this so-called purpose," Barry said, "I was still drinking and smoking and cutting up and getting into fights, and I wasn't putting in any extra time on the courts. Clearly I wasn't committed to the game, and I wasn't pursuing it as a purpose. I see now that what was happening was that I was learning that basketball wasn't my real calling in life and I lacked passion. I'd been playing since I was ten, and I thought that basketball was the only area in which I could ever excel. But that was just circumstances. My real purpose was soon to come." He was conducting good, honest introspection, a key for personal development, and beginning a positive success trajectory.

Up until this point, he had been behind during much of his formal education. "In high school, I had my share of Ds and Fs," Barry said. "College was not easy for me, but I managed Cs and a few Bs once I got to my major of physical education. Then once it became clear that I wasn't going to be rich and famous playing basketball, I figured I would coach, which would allow me to pursue my love of basketball." But when even his enthusiasm for basketball as a sport began to wane, Barry was left adrift.

Luckily for him, Michele encouraged him to take an economics class with her. The class was a turning point in his life. "Wow, talk about a great professor and a great subject!" he said. "Our professor, Dr. Sam Spector, was tremendously enthusiastic, and he had a way of making it all come alive. Yes, economics—guns and butter—and the whole nine yards." Almost in an instant, Barry developed a love for learning and understood the power of learning, and he began to see where his true purpose lay.

Barry changed his major to business and his grades improved, and upon graduation he enrolled in the MBA program at Stetson University in Florida. As usual, he worked his way through school. He remained with the same trucking company, and to accommodate his class schedule, he worked the overnight shift. He'd work from 11:00 P.M. to 7:00 A.M. in Orlando, drive back to DeLand and attend classes, do his homework, catch a little sleep, and then drive back to Orlando and repeat the process.

The next step in solidifying his purpose unexpectedly arrived when Barry received the terrible news that his father, after years of struggling with alcoholism, had committed suicide. Barry was in his last semester of graduate school when he was called out of class and given the news. "Rather than the usual role of helping family members deal with the loss and making funeral arrangements," Barry said, "my brother and I had to deal with the loss from a different perspective. While trying to be there for family as they grieved, we also had to deal with lots of financial burdens, as my father had no insurance and quite a bit of debt. In fact, we had to take out loans to deal with the burial and debts left behind." The experience left an indelible mark on Barry. Little did he know that it would plant the seeds of a passion for life insurance and a purpose that would carry him through a long career. "Thank goodness for insurance," he said, "and for insurance agents who work so hard to help people avoid this situation whenever possible."

Astonishingly, a few years later Barry's stepfather also died from alcoholism. Both deaths were sudden, and Barry did not wish to go into detail about either. He merely said that both losses "hit close to home" and were "very difficult to handle."

After earning a master's degree in finance in less than two

years, Barry accepted a position in a management development program at Metropolitan Life Insurance Company (MetLife).

Continued Human Capital Building
While Pursuing a Career

Over the next ten years, steady promotions took Barry and his family all over the country, including stops in Atlanta; New York City, twice; Tampa and Lakeland, Florida; Chattanooga; and Birmingham. He last served as CEO of MetLife Marketing Corporation just prior to joining The Principal Financial Group® in Des Moines, Iowa, in 1988 as an agency vice president. At The Principal® he was promoted to senior vice president in 1991, executive vice president in 1996, president in 1998, CEO in 2000, and then chairman in 2002.

When asked how he rose to a level in a company where he could have such an impact, Barry's response was matter-of-fact. "I really never set out to serve as CEO of a large company," he said. "But upon reflection, I can see that getting to that position has been a lifelong journey, with one building block being added at a time—one door opened another. And overcoming adversity played a significant role, not only in becoming CEO but in all of my life and career. One of the negative consequences of an upbringing like mine is that I was left with a feeling of inferiority—and that feeling was hard to shake. In every situation I encountered, I felt as though I was the least qualified, and plenty of times, I probably was! But I always had a strong work character, and I worked extra hard to compensate for any deficiencies, imagined or real. Then, once I found my purpose, I always tried to do the very best at whatever I was asked to do. Eventually, success breeds success, and your mind starts to accept it."

Still, remaining on an upward trajectory wasn't always easy, and Barry is the first to admit that he has fallen a time or two. Barry recalls his first significant management position. He was appointed district manager for MetLife's Lakeland, Florida, office at the age of twenty-nine. As was generally the case, the opportunity to take over a sales office came about because the office was underperforming. "I took over a struggling office, and my first task was to interview the four sales managers in the office," he said. "As I interviewed the first three managers, each resigned on the spot. I was at a brand-new job, and three-fourths of my team had just walked out on me. As you can imagine, I was deathly afraid to interview the last manager—especially as he was the one who thought he should have gotten the job as district manager! Luckily, we hit it off and he stayed. We actually became great friends as we built the Lakeland district into one of the top performers in the country."

Later, he took on a new position in Alabama that placed him over four hundred agents and thirty managers. At his first sales conference he had to address them as a group, and to say the least, public speaking was not his forte. "Back when I was regional VP at MetLife," Barry said, "I'd do anything possible to get out of public speaking! But here in this brand-new position, where I'd been sent off to create a new region, there was no avoiding it." He worked extra hard on a motivational speech, and he came off the stage feeling that it had gone reasonably well. His boss, however, had a different take. "That was the worst speech I've ever heard!" he said, and he wasn't joking. "My speech may not have been *that* bad," Barry said, laughing, "but I took the comment to heart and knew I would need to work to become a good speaker." Barry went on to get professional coaching in public speaking and has become a top-notch speaker.

Adversity on the Job

Barry became CEO of The Principal in 2000. The Principal, a leading global financial company, offers business, individual, and institutional clients a wide range of financial products and services. It may be best known as the nation's largest 401(k) plan administrator. When Barry became the CEO, the Principal was a 121-year-old mutual insurance company with 16,000 employees and a market capitalization or value equivalent to about $6.8 billion. The term "mutual" identifies a company that was established to serve and be controlled by its members—policyholders in this case—and is a business structure that is becoming less and less common around the world.

Throughout most of 2000 and early 2001 Barry and his management team put an incredible amount of work and time into preparing to take Principal from a mutual company into a much more nimble and capable public corporation. The process of taking mutual insurance companies public is more commonly known as demutualization. When companies go public, there is a tremendous amount of planning and preparation involved, and one of the last steps in the process is conducting what the industry calls "road shows." Road shows promote the company so that, when they do go public, individual and institutional investors buy their stock. In this case it meant selling roughly $2 billion of a $6.8 billion company at the opening bell of the stock market on a given day. Prior members, the mutual policyholders, were offered stock or cash in exchange for their part-membership in the mutual company. Barry and his team had planned on a scheduled launch on the New York Stock Exchange of October 1, 2001.

In early September 2001, Barry and his team conducted a dry run at the World Trade Center and received feedback from various investment banks. Days later they flew to Paris to start the initial public offering (IPO) and to conduct their European road show, which was to be followed by two weeks of touring in the United States. Barry had the television on in his hotel room as he was getting dressed, and as he was about to leave for the first meeting, he saw a troubling image on the screen: smoke rising from one of Manhattan's Twin Towers. "I assumed there had been some terrible accident," he said, "that a small plane had accidentally hit the tower." He hurried on to his meeting, and it was there that he discovered the enormity and tragedy of what was happening back home.

"The tragedy of 9/11 and being out of the country when it happened is beyond comprehension and description," Barry said. "All I could think about was getting home—to family and coworkers. Certainly my focus on the demutualization process and the road show no longer dominated my thoughts and energies. My problems were minuscule relative to others who were directly impacted by the terrorist attacks, those who were killed and those who lost loved ones." The IPO was immediately canceled, and Barry and his colleagues began making arrangements to return home. U.S. airspace, however, was closed indefinitely, so the team found themselves stranded in Paris.

On September 13, still grounded in Europe with no foreseeable way to get home, where his family and his company needed him most, Barry and his team learned that the Canadian border was opening for air traffic and would provide ground access into the United States. He quickly tried to charter a plane. Naturally, this was a challenge in itself, since so many stranded passengers were trying to get home and air travel was severely restricted. But he learned that it was possible to fly to Iceland and then on to Winnipeg, where they'd then try to procure ground transportation.

After sitting in Reykjavik for hours, they flew to Winnipeg, where the airport authorities were not at all thrilled to have a private aircraft from outside of Canada landing at their airport. Barry and crew were taken into custody, sequestered, and interrogated at the airport before being released to go on their way hours later. He and several other executives then rented a van and a driver for the overnight drive back to headquarters in Des Moines. But the long journey was not over. Late into the night, with passengers asleep, the driver fell asleep at the wheel in South Dakota. The van went off the road and struck several barriers, and the windshield caved in. Fortunately no one was hurt. They drove to a 7-Eleven and got help.

Finally, Barry gratefully returned to Des Moines, and while he may have wanted to take a few days to recover and to be with family, the need to regroup and replan the IPO demanded his immediate attention. "We did a lot of soul-searching and a lot of talking with bankers," he said, "and in the end we decided to give it a shot."

Moving Forward, a Pattern for Overcoming Adversity

The New York Stock Exchange reopened on September 17 and ended the week with the Dow Jones Industrial Average down nearly 1,370 points, a decline of 14 percent and at the time the worst five-day performance since the Great Depression. The

Principal stuck to its objective however, and rescheduled its public offering. "We wanted to pave the way for financial companies to get back on track," Barry said. On October 23 The Principal became the first major company to go public on Wall Street following 9/11. Principal and its employees made a large charitable contribution to the 9/11 relief fund that same day, and the IPO was a great success. "It was very well received," Barry said. "Oversubscribed, in fact."

Since going public in 2001 The Principal has experienced solid growth both in assets under management and profitability. Efforts to make the company more profitable actually started in 1998, when operating earnings were $267 million. They increased every year up until 2007, when earnings topped $1 billion at year-end 2007. At the close of 2001, The Principal managed $98 billion, and that number topped $300 billion prior to the financial markets crisis that was sparked by the subprime debacle in 2008.

The period since September 2001 has been one of the most challenging in business history. In addition to the events surrounding 9/11, we've seen major recessions as well as escalation in debt defaults due to fraud, corruption, and mismanagement. We've seen well-known companies like Enron, Arthur Andersen, WorldCom, Tyco, United Airlines, and Conseco all fall apart, which brought on the enactment of the Sarbanes-Oxley Act. We've seen wars in Afghanistan and Iraq and disasters like the tsunami in Asia and hurricanes on the Gulf Coast, and we are still suffering from the repercussions of the more recent subprime and related credit markets problems which have reached global proportions, and which continue to add to an already long list of iconic companies that have fallen.

Under Barry's leadership, The Principal weathered a number of these large-scale storms, and he helped prepare the company to withstand the market upheavals we've seen in 2008. He accomplished a great deal over a short period of time and made The Principal exponentially more profitable, but profit isn't what brings him the most fulfillment. "What I'm really proud of," he said, "is The Principal being named one of the one hundred best companies to work for by *Fortune* magazine for the last seven years. The Principal has won many customer-service awards and received the Spirit of America Award from the United Way of America for our contributions to the community. Having great performance is wonderful, but that needs to be accompanied by giving your customers great value and excellent service, treating employees well, and giving back to your communities."

Adversity and Business Go Hand in Hand

To all appearances, the 2001 public launch of The Principal and the ringing of the New York Stock Exchange opening bell on October 23, 2001, were euphoric events for Barry and The Principal. It was indeed a momentous occasion, but what the public did not know was that, behind the scenes, Barry and upper management were facing an entirely different kind of adversity.

In 1999, with Barry as president and following a strategy to expand their retirement services business globally, The Principal made an offer to purchase BT Australia, a financial services company about one-quarter the size of The Principal, for approximately $1.4 billion. "Australia had a mandatory retirement system," Barry said. "We saw it as an incredible opportunity."

The Principal didn't have the leading bid, but as it turned out, there was a cultural conflict between the company with the leading bid and BT management. So, as Barry put it, "The Principal was there to sweep up."

But in the end the "incredible opportunity" didn't deliver. The integration of BT Australia into The Principal did not go well and the envisioned synergies never occurred, and at the same time the fundamentals of the market changed. "A number of things didn't go as planned or desired," Barry said. "For one, the market there was not The Principal's core business. The banks in Australia decided they wanted to dominate this area, and we were at a competitive disadvantage. And the exchange rate [for the dollar] fell precipitously."

Understandably, Barry and The Principal were under constant pressure from stock analysts to address the BT issue. "There was tremendous pressure to do something with the underachieving asset," Barry said. "We were now a public company, and we'd implemented new processes such as required quarterly conference calls with investors and analysts—we had a lot of people to answer to."

The Principal decided to take action. They sold BT Australia in 2002 for a loss of more than $500 million, which was more than The Principal had ever made as profits in a year. Problems with equity markets and local consolidation by the banks made it a buyer's market, making the bad situation even worse. Businesses often do not survive such situations intact, and the chances of their leader surviving are even less. But Barry had been learning how to pick himself up by the bootstraps all his life. Now he needed to help pick up an entire company. He did this not by looking for scapegoats and firing them, but by putting together teams to analyze what they had done right and what they had done wrong. They designed a new map for going forward.

Rather than focus on mature competitive markets, Barry and his team started to sharpen their focus on emerging markets, where retirement savings would provide a growth engine, such as Brazil, India, China, and Malaysia. The strategy worked even better than expected: By year-end 2001, The Principal's international division was managing $3.7 billion, and by year-end 2007 that amount had reached $28.7 billion. Further, Barry didn't miss the opportunity to learn from the experience and improve his own leadership skills. "I was personally and emotionally involved in this acquisition," he said. "I spent two years traveling back and forth from Des Moines to Australia trying to make it work, which obviously I wanted very badly. One of the best lessons I learned was that no matter how personally invested you are, as a leader you have to be willing to make tough decisions, to take decisive action when it needs to be taken."

Because neither The Principal as a whole nor Barry as its leader would lie down and succumb to this significant adversity, but use it to become savvier, smarter, and even more effective, it was possible to recover from even a $500 million mistake. And The Principal certainly showed no concern about Barry's leadership: He bought BT as president, and sold it as CEO.

Horatio Alger Association

Over the years, Barry has been fortunate enough to receive many awards recognizing his business savvy. The award he values most was bestowed upon him in 2003, when he was inducted into the Horatio Alger Association of Distinguished Americans. The organization, which was founded in 1947, honors the achievements of individuals who have attained success in spite of major life obstacles. It also supports higher education by bestowing scholarships upon promising students who have overcome adversity. In 2007 the association contributed approximately $12 million in scholarships. To date there are more than five hundred Horatio Alger members, and they're some of the most business-savvy people in the world. Most of them, like Barry, come from the most humble of beginnings. They include noted businesspeople such as T. Boone Pickens, Wayne Huizenga, Rick Hendrick, Truett Cathy, and John Pappajohn, in addition to distinguished persons such as Oprah Winfrey, Dr. Maya Angelou, Tom Brokaw, Herbert Hoover, and Norman Vincent Peale.

"As I stepped to the podium to make a few comments," Barry recalled, "I was overwhelmed with gratitude and pride. And the incredible thing about it was that my brother and mother, along with my own children, were there to experience it with me. As I said that night, in so many ways it was my mother who should have gotten the award. She's the one who overcame the worst adversity, and who has emerged from all of it with an optimistic attitude despite all she's been through."

The Individual Human Capital Profile

So what is it that this story of J. Barry Griswell, filled with adversity, teaches us? The journey that he followed to become CEO of a Fortune 500 company is truly a rags–to–riches story. His industry, associates, competitors, company board, employees, and friends see him as a very business-savvy person. To get to this point in his life he has defied all the odds. As a youth he was poor, his home was broken and learning was difficult. As an adult he fought medical issues and the occasional career setback. But he learned early on to persevere despite all the odds, and that ability has facilitated both personal and career success.

After many years of adversity and many years of success, he's in an excellent position to reflect upon how one achieves success in business. I asked him to comment upon each of the individual human capital components and how they contributed to his overall success:

Introspection: HC Component No. 1

Introspection is the practice of observing oneself—one's personality, strengths and weaknesses, overall performance, motivations, goals, ideas, and capabilities—and conducting honest self-assessments. Introspection is harder than it would at first seem, because being completely honest with oneself is no easy task. Some are loath to admit their faults, some have an exaggerated sense of self-worth or of a particular ability, and sometimes what we're truly capable of isn't at all reflected in our actual performance, making objective standards somewhat misleading. Being able to conduct truly honest introspection is a learned skill that becomes easier over time, after lots of practice.

As Barry's ability to conduct introspection grew, so did the rest of his human capital. Not until he really started to understand who he was and what he was capable of—which was far more than his difficult start would suggest—did his trajectory start to change. Introspection and the positive changes it leads us to make through focused improvement are a very significant part of business savvy. I asked Barry to comment on the value of introspection for human capital development.

"First let's think about the role of mirrors," Barry said. "I'm not talking about the looking glass we need for applying makeup or driving a car, but the inner mirror that allows us to see ourselves as we really are. What sets human beings apart from other species is our ability to see ourselves from outside ourselves—the ability to see ourselves as others see us. I believe that this unique ability is the catalyst for all human growth and development.

"By far the most important use of the mirror is introspection. Introspection allows us to look deep within and analyze our motives, priorities, and to measure our progress toward goals. Most important, introspection allows us to get an accurate measure of purpose, passion, and commitment to dreams and goals. To truly know oneself can be daunting, but it's essential in order to experience personal success."

Our self-understanding needs to be 100 percent accurate. We need an accurate read on our weak areas so we can direct our efforts to focused self-improvement and maintaining an upward success trajectory.

Values Behavior: HC Component No. 2

Barry's story highlights how values do not have to be compromised to get ahead. Good values, and behavior that matches those values, are paramount to maintaining a positive trajectory over long periods of time. Compromising values may get someone ahead in the short run but will always bring him down in the long run.

"I do not believe for a second that you can be a bad person— a dishonest or cruel person—and have true success," Barry said. "The kind of so-called success achieved this way cannot give you peace and contentment. This kind of success is temporal at best. A business slogan I really like is, 'Do the right things and do them right.' I firmly believe that honesty and integrity are the foundation for any type of success—honesty with others and, more important, honesty with oneself.

"To this day I try to live by the principle my mother taught me—to never, ever tell a lie. It's not easy. Sometimes the truth hurts and sometimes we think we know it when we don't. But that old saying is right: The truth, the real truth, will set you free. To me, truth is like the river running to the ocean. You can slow it, you can divert it, you can even dam it up and make a lake, but, in the end, it will always be known, and it will find its way to the ocean where everyone can see it."

The other part of values behavior that Barry finds especially important can be summed up with the deceptively simple saying "Who you are matters most." "I do believe there is a higher purpose in life," he said. "For me it's of a religious nature, but 'who you are matters most' applies to religious folks, agnostics, atheists, anybody. What I mean is that you need to know who you are at a fundamental, core level so you'll know what purpose it is you're meant to fulfill. I don't think you'll find true happiness or true success unless you're fulfilling your true purpose, your life's highest calling. Last, I have always found the concept of treating others as you would have them treat you to be a wonderful guiding principle."

Work Character: HC Component No. 3

In being business savvy there is no substitute for hard work. Barry gained a strong work character when he was young, and it never left him. He also demonstrated the need to gain new skills, such as effective public speaking, to supplement the hard work.

"There's no substitute for hard work," Barry said. "This can be a tough one for many people to accept, and when I include this in my speeches to young people, I always start by saying, 'My guess is that most of you really aren't going to like this one, but it's so true.' If you buy into the theory that success is about reaching your personal potential, about achieving stretch goals and doing it 'right,' there must be hard work. If this is true, why do so many think they can achieve success without hard work? Perhaps it's a reflection of our society—especially with TV shows, movies, commercials, and infomercials that constantly send a 'get-rich-quick' message.

"The widespread belief that money can be quickly and effortlessly made probably explains why the lottery system has taken off in this country. Why work hard to achieve financial success when you might win millions with the simple act of buying a lotto ticket? My home state's lotto message is, 'You have to play to win.' That may sound appealing, but the truth is, *you have to work to win.*

"I was fortunate to have had to work at a very young age. I got used to it early, and my work character has served me well in every type of job I've had."

Purpose and Passion: HC Component No. 4

"This next principle is magical," Barry said. "If hard work is critical, then we need to find a way to really enjoy our work so that it's no longer work but rather something we're passionate about. The trick is to view work as a means to far greater benefits or enjoyment.

"As will become apparent throughout this book, I now realize that I was fortunate to have grown up in an impoverished environment. I was the first person in my family to go to college. When I received my MBA and took my first job as an insurance agent, many were surprised, including my dear mother. Along the way I was asked countless times why I chose insurance as a career. My answer was, 'It gives me a purpose that transcends just doing a job.'

"I never forgot how badly we needed insurance after my father died suddenly, and how burdensome it was to be left with so much unexpected debt. What a noble cause it was, I thought, to help families protect themselves if the breadwinner were to die prematurely, to have an income should a disability occur, or to help someone plan for a secure retirement. Was selling life insurance boring? No way. I had a strong and exciting purpose.

"I found my purpose early and I pursued it with passion. Difficult at times? You bet. In fact, I'm sure I quit mentally or emotionally a hundred times my first few years selling insurance. But my purpose helped me keep going despite all the challenges."

Thirst for Knowledge: HC Component No. 5

"The power of knowledge and lifetime learning is transformative," Barry said. "I have no idea why it took so long for me to realize this. Perhaps it was because my early childhood development was lacking due to our circumstances.

"While it took me almost twenty years to catch up, my grades in college eventually became good enough to get an academic scholarship to supplement my athletic scholarship. I even managed to get into graduate school and earn an MBA while loading trucks at night. But most important, I learned the power of knowledge and how to acquire it. It's a habit I've maintained my entire adult life. Lifetime learning and an ongoing curiosity have been absolutely essential to my success."

The Adversity Paradox Takeaways:
Developing Your Human Capital

- As your individual human capital grows, your ability to cope with adversity may improve, but one thing we know for sure is that adversity will always be with us. As Barry's story and the stories of others in this book will show, not shying away from adversity but rather using it to bolster individual human capital development can take a trajectory bottomed out at the lowest low and turn it into one of great success.
- Review each of the five human capital components:
  — introspection
  — values behavior
  — work character
  — purpose and passion
  — thirst for knowledge

Are you particularly strong in any of them? Weak? If you find that you need improvement in any of the human capital components, take extra care to see how those we profile in the following chapters developed that particular area of their human capital.

3

The Power of "And Then Some":
The Connection Between Adversity,
Human Capital, and Business Savvy

We've now seen the adversity paradox in action in two great business leaders—John Pappajohn and J. Barry Griswell. John Pappajohn was the child of immigrants who came to this country with very little, and then his father, the family breadwinner, died when John was sixteen, leaving John to provide for two younger brothers and a mother who spoke no English. John, who had been working since he was a small child, threw himself into the family grocery business and helped keep the struggling family afloat. Later he put himself through school, and with a keen interest and talent for business, plus a tremendous work character already established, got his education and became one of the country's first venture capitalists. Further, he's one of the most successful. Many would be surprised to hear that he credits his early work experience—selling rags and working in the grocery store—as the foundation of his eventual success. As for Barry, anyone would expect that someone with as rough a start as his would've ended up discouraged or dejected, at the very least. But instead of letting adversity trample him, Barry rejected a position of passivity and used the very misfortunes that could've easily stopped him in his tracks to galvanize a stellar path to success. He doesn't claim that it was easy or quick, and he doesn't claim that he didn't at times get disheartened. But he did make an active choice not to get stuck in those times of discouragement, and because he thoroughly knew the alternative, he made a commitment to bettering his life, no matter what.

Those who choose to make adversity their friend don't enjoy hardships any more than the next person. But there is a world of difference between those who befriend adversity by overcoming it and learning from the experience, and those who give up at the first sign of an obstacle. Take it from us, or take it just from looking at the world around you: Adversity is going to happen, and usually in ways you could've never foreseen. Knowing this, make a choice right now to look at adversity in a new light the next time it comes your way. Though it may not look so friendly on the surface, realize that adversity is an ally and that it's here to teach you something of crucial importance. Of course it's an unwelcome visitor. But when it presents itself, treat the experience as a unique learning opportunity. Here is your chance to impact positively your human capital development in ways that no seminar, class, or training session can even closely approximate.

So how does a well-developed human capital that has been fortified by overcoming adversity specifically promote the development of business savvy? First, let's remember the five components of human capital: *introspection, values behavior, work character, purpose and passion,* and a *thirst for knowledge.* When fully developed, these components come together and form a synergistic package called the *business-savvy framework*—a package that enables the very core competencies that ensure success. Let's take "purpose and passion," for instance. Those who have developed purpose and passion are so committed in their endeavors that they have an uncommon perseverance, as well as a commitment that goes well beyond the job. If you've found your purpose and passion, work is no longer work. You're fully engaged and can't wait to get to the office and devote your time to what you love. These people continually have visions of what the future might hold, and fortitude when the going gets really tough. They can conceive an objective and execute it, and they do so with boundless enthusiasm and motivation that naturally bubbles up from within, because they're living out the purpose that gives their lives and careers meaning. With this kind of attitude, superior performance is nearly guaranteed.

It works this way with each of the human capital components. A vibrant thirst for knowledge, for instance, will naturally drive you to seek out information and continually stay on top of your game. Again, the well-informed worker who knows his job inside and out is in a far better position to deliver a superior performance than a colleague who is indifferent or even resistant to learning, or who, when he encounters a serious information void, gives up, gets discouraged, or passes the buck to someone else. Likewise, a person with well-developed skills of introspection will always know her strengths and weaknesses, and thus be able to apply her strengths to whatever business she's in as well as do whatever it takes to ameliorate the weaknesses. This kind of employee is already ahead of the game. This is how it works with each of the human capital components: Your human capital naturally drives the development of the very core competencies that create and sustain success. And just think of what you can accomplish when you've fully developed each component of individual human capital!

The fully developed business-savvy framework will vary slightly from person to person, but this chart gives a good idea of what it could look like:

The Business-Savvy Framework

COMPONENTS of Human Capital			
Introspection			
Self-understanding Strengths and weaknesses Focused improvement Constant use of mirrors and mentors			
Values Behavior			
Ethical grounding that steers and guides a person			
	Work Character		
	Disciplined and personally effective, with some urgency		
		Purpose and Passion	
		Mission focused	
			Thirst for Knowledge
			Ability to synthesize, developed through continuous learning
Honesty	Time management	Tenacity	Formal and informal education
Integrity	Communication	Fortitude	Experiential learning
Trust	Decision-making	Perseverance	Inquisitiveness
Openness	Organization	Commitment	World exploration
Care for others	Teamwork	Confidence	Innovation
Acceptance	Accountability	Fearlessness	Intellectual curiosity
Forgiveness	Delegation	Optimism	Lifelong learning
Core COMPETENCIES			
			• Systems and linear thinking, in depth knowledge • Understanding information gaps and voids
		• Vision of achieving purpose-driven goals • Courage to pursue against all odds	
	• "And Then Some", the work ethic portion of work character • Dialogue and discussion - key tools in working with others		
• Self-respect and respect for others • Empathy, a broader view for dealing with dilemmas			

The temptation will be to jump immediately down to the end result: Can't a person just adopt the core competencies we list here? Unfortunately, our years of experience and our research have told us there are no shortcuts. We don't even have a fancy acronym so the core competencies can be easily memorized— save that for the one-day seminar taught by the motivational guru. You won't find any shortcuts here, but we will tell you how to use the "trial by fire" of overcoming adversity to build your human capital efficiently and gain the business savvy needed to earn success.

But it's one thing to know you should befriend adversity, and entirely another to actually do it, no? *How* does one accomplish this very difficult task, one that, quite understandably, most people avoid? When we first began discussing the concepts of this book we knew there was a powerful force common among those who are truly successful, a power that seems to be routine for some but latent for most. It's one of the best and simplest ways we know to start befriending adversity. It's also one of the most powerful.

The Key to Befriending Adversity: The Amazing Power of "And Then Some"

During Barry's high school years of working for the trucking company, he was part of a group of part-time employees the company turned to when things got especially busy. Rather than adding permanent jobs or paying overtime to regular employees to cover a worker who was on vacation or out sick, the trucking company would use students and moonlighters to fill its needs.

These jobs were highly sought after as they paid extremely well. One night loading trucks gave Barry more than he made in a week as a lifeguard, and a weekend might cover a month's financial needs. Most of the time there were far more people wanting to work than were needed, so Barry's goal was to work his way to the top of the call list. To get to the top, it was important to take the work whenever called, but Barry quickly discovered that going above and beyond, putting in some extra work, was the way to *remain* at the top. Extra work might mean staying later to get a truck loaded or unloaded, or more than carrying his weight on a crew.

Whatever the goal, Barry made sure he met it and then routinely *surpassed* it. In other words, he met the goal or expectation, and then gave a little more—every single time. Maybe it meant staying past quitting time to finish a job. Maybe it meant volunteering for the tough assignments nobody else wanted. Maybe it meant being willing to work holidays. Whatever it was, this little extra made the difference between being at the top of the call list and the middle, and it differentiated him from all the others. In no time at all, he came to be known as the guy who could be counted on to go above and beyond. "And then some" also made a tangible difference in Barry's lifestyle. The income generated by "and then some" was critical during a period in which he simply did not have the cash to support the most meager of lifestyles. It got him and his family over the threshold of survival.

Eventually, Barry began applying the practice of "and then some" to everything he attempted. "My experience at the trucking company taught me the importance of giving work your all and then some," he said. "I may not have known I was learning it at the time, but doing my very best *and then some* has become one of the most important means of my success throughout my career, no matter what job I was in. I know of no better way to quickly distinguish yourself at work, at home, in your community, or in civil service, than when asked to do something, do what is asked *and then some.*"

Bob's first understanding of the power of "and then some" came later in life, but like Barry's it was driven by the need for a means of survival and occurred at a critical crossroad. He had worked full-time in the summers since eighth grade, generating the cash that provided some of the nicer things a teenager might enjoy. With the money he saved he was able to purchase his own car and occasional trips to the ski slopes with buddies. It was not until after college, when he went into commission-based sales, that Bob found himself in a position in which something had to change or failure was imminent.

The job entailed selling equipment to construction contractors. During his first six months on the job, Bob sold nothing. Like many young people he had little in reserve and serious bills to pay, and soon enough he was pulling money out of pocket in order to work—not uncommon for many as they test the waters of commission-based sales.

Something had to change, and quickly. Although Bob didn't describe it in those words at the time, he started implementing the power of "and then some." He started showing up on construction sites at six A.M. when the gates opened, meeting customers late at night when they would be putting in a bid early the next morning, and thoroughly vetting sales presentations with coworkers ahead of making sales calls. As his presentation skills improved, he gained more confidence. He made a habit of working harder than his peers and surpassing his boss's expectations. In the next six months, Bob went from deficit spending to an annual income many don't see in a lifetime.

We both discovered early in our careers that the success gained by using the power of "and then some" was really just the tip of the iceberg. Like the others we studied, the results of "and then some" in business were undeniable: It gave us an advantage over the competition and earned us reputations as hard workers who could be counted on to get the job done and to do it right. It helped create a solid work character. But its true power lies in employing the principle of "and then some" as a way of life. We began to use it in all arenas of our lives—work, sports, hobbies, even relationships. And when adversity struck, we knew just where to turn.

When we encountered a setback, we applied the power of "and then some" to self-improvement. Nothing could stop us from conducting some introspection, identifying the particular weakness (or in some instances, weaknesses) that had contributed to the adversity, and laboring relentlessly to remedy it. In some cases, the improvements generated by "and then some" even caused a weakness to turn into a strength. Barry delivered a terrible speech. So he set to work on becoming a better public speaker, bolstered his public speaking skills, and became one of the most engaging speakers you'll ever hear. Bob had a terrible sales record. So he identified his weak areas, practiced his sales presentations so he could anticipate and answer every possible objection the buyer could make, put in longer days than his competition, and became one of the company's top producers.

Of course, there are certain forms of adversity that are in no way attributable to any personal fault or weakness or could even be caused by an honest mistake. The death of a loved one, for example, or a major health crisis or injury, would be difficult for anyone, and there's no way we can be thoroughly prepared for such things. Being born into humble circumstances, or being laid off, or being in the midst of an economic recession are also adversities that affect us through no fault of our own. Clearly some hardships are worse than others, but if you're relying on the power of "and then some" as an overarching attitude, as an entire way of life, you've got access to a deep and abiding source of fortitude that you can count on to help you through even the worst adversity. If you haven't noticed it already, let us point out one of the great things about "and then some": *You are the agent of change.* In other words, the power to act, to change your own circumstances positively, lies with you. No matter how difficult the circumstances, relying on and harnessing the power of "and then some" ensures that you're never helpless in the face of adversity.

As "and then some" is a universal principle, you can apply it to any manner of adversity you encounter. Have you been laid off? Start with a goal of targeting five companies a day and then find five more, and don't rest until you follow through by contacting the person in charge of hiring or by sending your résumé. Are you faced with an information void that's preventing you from achieving your goals? Determine the best way to fill that void, and then go above and beyond in terms of your research; don't stop until you've mastered that particular topic. Are you weak in a particular area, such as public speaking, making cold calls, team leadership, or even a software program? Do whatever it takes to gain not only competency but also proficiency in whatever area is holding you back from reaching your potential.

"And then some" certainly applies to adversities or challenges beyond the business arena as well. So many people these days, for example, are trying to lose weight or commit to a workout routine, or both. Harnessing the power of "and then some" is the perfect tool for such goals. Set your goal, do everything you can to achieve it no matter how tired or unmotivated you feel, and next week or month, set your goal a little higher. One of the wonderful things about "and then some" is that if you're truly meeting your goals and then surpassing them, the amazing results you'll achieve will be an extremely powerful motivational force. Success breeds success. We believe that if you habitually use the power of "and then some" to build your human capital, you'll find that the positive results will surpass all your expectations.

One of the greatest things about the power of "and then some" is that it's available to all of us—people of every age, every profession, every educational level, every level of experience. No special skills are necessary—just the willingness to learn from adversity and to put in some extra effort. And if you're lucky enough not to have experienced full-scale adversity, you can start by applying the power of "and then some" to all the setbacks, obstacles, and even daily nuisances that will always arise in business.

The Power Resides in All of Us

There are a few who seem to have a natural proclivity for employing the power of "and then some," but for most of us, it takes work to get good at it. Maybe you've seen the power of "and then some" at work among your own acquaintances or even in yourself. Or maybe you know people who are good at something but you're not sure why. Let us suggest that it's very likely they're

drawing on the power of "and then some." As we started targeting and profiling those who came from humble beginnings so we
could best understand the power and see it at work, we began to
recognize it in many of the people right next door or just down
the hall. Word of what we were writing about didn't need to
spread far before we heard story after story of adversities overcome, of people who had learned to implement the power of "and
then some." Friends, coworkers, and even members of the think
tank we'd put together to help guide our pursuit of a better understanding all offered up stories of themselves or others who,
when faced with adversity, chose not to wallow in self-pity or be
struck down by adversity but to combat its negative repercussions with the power of "and then some."

One of our good friends is Duane Gibson, a Baptist pastor
and one of the few not in the realm of business to have a strong
influence on this book. It wasn't our intent when we began our
research to use nonbusiness stories, but Duane's was so compelling, and so validated our beliefs about what creates success
and the critical nature that adversity can play, we thought we
would share a few tidbits here.

Duane was born in the projects north of downtown Chicago
in 1940. His father, whom he has never met, left before he was
born. His mother was raised in an orphanage and achieved only
an eighth-grade education. Duane had four siblings, all by different fathers. The family was totally dependent on government
welfare programs and social services and their claim to fame was
being a "model" welfare family.

Duane, however, never let the adversities in his life stop him.
In fact, he doesn't even use the word "adversity," preferring instead to describe the misfortunes and major setbacks in his life

as "learning experiences." Further, and this is very important, he made an active *choice* to see each of his "learning experiences" as positives. We don't mean that Duane was living in a fantasy world or that he didn't experience grief or pain—in fact, Duane is as well grounded and realistic as they come. He simply found a positive in every situation. He didn't, for instance, dwell on his mother's lack of education, but thought of how she was an avid reader and how they spent every other Friday afternoon at the library. He didn't dwell on the fact that he grew up in the projects, but chose to focus on the fun and community he found in the project playgrounds. And somehow he looked at intact families not with envy but with admiration.

Duane earned a football scholarship to Wake Forest University but dropped out after a year, feeling that he did not fit in with his new peers. Back in Chicago he became more involved with his church, and his pastor encouraged him to give school another try. Then a deacon in the church offered to pay his first semester's tuition. Duane enrolled in college and got a degree in sociology, and followed it up with a master's degree from the Jane Addams Graduate School at the University of Illinois in Chicago. Along the way he worked with social work programs, including a Jewish community center and a school for kids with disabilities, and he did leadership work with Urban Ministries helping gang kids. Duane's objectives and education were built around social work, and through his work he came to understand that kids making a religious connection were greatly improving their chances in life. He felt the need to combine his social work with religious work.

So the kid who'd dropped out of college and then returned for a bachelor's and a master's went back to school again. He completed two years of seminary, and then became a probation officer in Cook County, Illinois, and dealt with delinquent kids on Chicago's South Side. One of his assigned kids, Jerome, was being pressured to join a gang, and with Duane's support he resisted. But the pressure on Jerome persisted, and one day he was stripped of his shoes and socks and forced to walk home in the snow. Later he even received a facial wound from a shotgun blast. At this point Duane realized that despite all the support he could muster for Jerome, the gang wasn't going to let up, and their efforts were only going to become more violent. As Duane saw it, Jerome had only one option, at least for the time being. "Do what you have to do to survive," he counseled Jerome.

Losing Jerome to a gang was a terrible blow to Duane, one of his most painful adversities. He'd failed to do the job he'd set out to do, and a kid's future was on the line.

But Duane knew that he had a choice in how to view and deal with this failure, and he chose not to let it stop or even inhibit his efforts. In fact, the failure became a key learning opportunity for Duane, and relying on the power of "and then some," he did everything in his power to reap some good from the painful experience and prevent it from happening again. One of his most important realizations was that the best way to help at-risk kids like Jerome was to intervene well before they found themselves at such a dire point. He turned his attention to *prevention,* to giving these kids healthy alternatives, giving them enough to live for and enough support so that joining a gang was not the obvious and only survival path. He also learned that even for kids in Jerome's situation, there are always alternatives.

And ultimately, the adversity of failure led Duane to his purpose in life: Duane committed himself to working with kids like Jerome. He worked for Special Education of Lake County, serving kids with disabilities, and taught at the Salvation Army training center in Chicago; then for two years he ran a youth facility for abandoned and neglected children. After that, he was offered a job as the associate pastor of his church. Suddenly all his experiences—serving at-risk youth, social justice, the ministry—coalesced and he knew he'd found his purpose with passion and the career path he would follow the rest of his life. Duane brought everything he'd learned from making adversity his friend and growing from it to bear upon his profession. He brought a deep well of compassion, empathy, and patience. He served as a senior pastor for more than twenty-five years, during which time he championed the cause of serving the less fortunate.

"People are hurting, often as a result of circumstances they are born into," Duane said. "The message I want to deliver is that you're never stuck. You have choices, and you can choose to be a victim of your circumstances or you can choose to change them. Adversity is never the end point; for those faced with a positive attitude, it's always the beginning."

A person we came to admire and respect greatly and who vividly demonstrates that adversity is never the end but only the beginning is Sheila Holzworth, a Principal Financial Group employee. She works in the human resources department and teaches people how to be assertive. She trains employees to be more like herself. Sheila defines determination, even though her world has been literally dark since she was ten years old. Fitted with orthodontic headgear as a child, the braces popped out of her mouth and the rubber bands caused the headgear to act like a slingshot. The braces were projected into her eyes and in an instant, Sheila was blinded. The loss of her sight was devastating, but with her family's encouragement, her strong faith, a positive attitude, and her early implementation of the power of "and then some," she picked up the challenge and never stopped.

Sheila, in fact, took up running. Others guided her during races with the use of radio frequency signals. In one race she got off course and wiped out five hurdles. Not even that stopped her. It soon became clear that she would spend her life breaking different kinds of barriers. Sheila was the first blind person in her elementary and high school, her college, and at The Principal. She broke records in water skiing and downhill skiing, and at the age of nineteen, Sheila reached the peak of her athletic career with a climb of Mount Rainier. In the thirty-six years since then, she's continued to overcome stereotypes and climb the corporate ladder.

We have also seen many other current and former coworkers with the power of "and then some." Larry Jorn has risen to be vice president of Baker Concrete, the largest specialty concrete contractor in the United States. Baker Concrete employs more than 3,000, and besides holding a number of records and firsts in its field, it has built more than twenty-five stadiums and arenas, including the homes of the Baltimore Colts, the Denver Broncos, and the Cincinnati Bengals. Larry's current success is a far cry from his early days living a somewhat reckless lifestyle.

Out of high school he went to work as a carpenter. One night he was out partying at the bars with friends and after having had a bit too much to drink got in a fight over a pool game. An assailant pulled a knife on him, and he was stabbed. Larry found himself in a local hospital's intensive care unit, where he would remain for a week, lucky to be alive.

There would be a number of other adversities later in Larry's life, but this early misfortune and his reflection on it best sums up his engagement of the power of "and then some." "The brush with death made me reevaluate my priorities, and I committed myself to going above and beyond my knee-jerk reaction to the stabbing," he said. "Instead of feeling sorry for myself and getting hung up on my injuries, I felt fortunate to be alive. Instead of focusing on revenge, I focused on getting well. Instead of blaming the other guy, I looked inward and recognized that my own actions had contributed to the problem." Larry chose not to let this serious setback stop him in any way and to focus instead on what he could control and change in going forward. It would be a routine he would employ time and again for the rest of his life.

Another former coworker who learned the power of "and then some" from an experience with adversity is Gene Postma. Out of high school Gene gave community college a shot before being lured away by the attractive hourly wages of a construction job. The job became a career, and after ten years Gene found himself running a crew and remodeling a building in New York City. The remodel included removing several layers of shingles on a steeply pitched roof. Gene was exasperated with his crew's slow progress and uneasiness on the roof, so he decided to demonstrate that there was nothing to worry about. Starting at the roof's peak, Gene started ripping and tearing when, all of a sudden, one of his toeholds broke loose, sending him sliding down the steep slope and off the edge into a twenty-five-foot fall. On the way down he shattered his arm on a balcony, and when he landed he incurred compression fractures in his back.

Gene's arm was pieced back together with a ten-inch metal plate and fourteen screws. Unfortunately, nothing could be done for his back. The doctors told him he would never be able to swing a hammer or run a trowel again. He was married with a two-year-old son and was unable to continue with his career.

It's at this point that many people would choose to give up. "But I wanted more," Gene said. "I wanted to continue being productive. And although my options were now severely limited, I realized I still had *options*." So he chose to participate in a government retraining program that would cover his college tuition if he returned to school. It wasn't easy. He had been gone from academia a long time, and he started out in entry-level classes that didn't qualify for graduation. Plus, money was very tight. But through the power of "and then some," Gene accepted the unexpected turn in his life and went back to school, put in extra effort with the books, and he and his wife both worked throughout his higher education to support the family. He graduated second in his class in less than four years with an engineering degree. He is now president of Western States Fire Protection Company, based in Denver, Colorado. The company has 1,500 employees and more than $200 million in annual sales. Like so many, Gene had the power of "and then some" before his fall, but adversity put it to work to grow his human capital well beyond that which he'd originally thought himself capable.

Another business acquaintance of ours is Suku Radia, former CFO of Meredith Corporation, a publishing and broadcasting company employing more than 3,000 and with $1.7 billion in annual sales. He is now the CEO of Bankers Trust Company, the largest locally owned bank in Iowa. In 1971 Suku came to the United States from Uganda to pursue a college degree. His great-grandparents had immigrated to Uganda from India, and his father was a successful Ugandan entrepreneur dealing in life insurance, real estate, and export brokering. Suku's family was well-off, so he'd led a relatively good life before coming to America.

But while he was in college, all of his family's wealth, including his college support, was taken by Idi Amin when the military dictator forcibly removed the entrepreneurial minority from Uganda. "I was left almost penniless in a foreign land," Suku said. "But I remained committed to completing my education, so I finished my business degree in two and a half years. I graduated with just $4.87 in my pocket." Starting from scratch, he took an entry-level job as a tax accountant with KPMG, and eventually he became a managing partner. From there he joined the Meredith Corporation as CFO in 2000, and, just this past year, was invited to take over the top position at Bankers Trust Company.

Perhaps the most amazing example of the power of "and then some" we came across most recently. At a United Way event, the entertainment was a man who was born in Nicaragua with eleven toes, a clubfoot, and no arms. His name is Tony Melendez. What was he doing? Playing the guitar and singing. He had learned to play the guitar—and very, very well we might add—with his feet and his toes. In fact, he is a renowned guitarist.

You probably know of similar examples of overcoming adversity, and some may even be your own. An educational setback, a physical injury, a career disruption, or the death of someone very close to you or on whom you are dependent all have the potential to derail a success trajectory. Thankfully, there is the power of "and then some." Harnessing the power starts with choosing not to make an enemy of adversity but a friend. The next step is actually applying the basic principle of "and then some" to everything you do. Put in the extra effort above and beyond others at work, and then expand the principle into a full cycle of self-improvement. We think you'll find, as we did, that bringing the power of "and then some" to everything you do will have an immeasurable positive impact on the development of your human capital. And a fully developed individual human capital makes for increased business savvy, and therefore success—success you may have never believed possible.

And just think—it all started with adversity.

Multiplying the Power of "And Then Some"

There's no doubt that using "and then some" on the micro level—harnessing its power in order to complete tasks and objectives—will produce terrific results. So then consider how powerful it could be on the macro level, or in applying the power of "and then some" to the whole process of self-improvement. To use "and then some" in such a manner, there is one crucial prerequisite: You must face adversity with a positive frame of mind.

The power of positive thinking has been well documented. These days, the psychology and self-help shelves of any bookstore are sagging with books on how a positive or optimistic attitude can help you succeed at anything from relationships, to career, to diet and exercise, to influencing people, to being a good parent. Well, having a positive attitude alone doesn't ensure any kind of success, but there's no denying that the optimists are, for the most part, far ahead of the pessimists. Optimists tend to do better with academics, in the workplace, and as members of sports teams or civic organizations. They also tend to have healthier relationships, and they're physically healthier, too—studies have shown that optimists visit the doctor far less often than pessimists, and that they have longer life spans.

In business we see the power of an optimistic attitude every day. Coworkers who maintain a positive attitude routinely produce better numbers or results than expected. Likewise, coworkers who accept the issues an adversity or major setback have created and tackle them by optimistically setting about learning and growing from the experience fare far better and travel much further down the success continuum than their pessimistic counterparts, who more often than not face adversity with an "Oh well, that's just the hand that fate dealt me" attitude. When adversity enters your life, you're faced with two basic choices, as shown below. The first is the optimist's choice: Accept the situation and then, harnessing the power of "and then some," analyze the situation to see what you can control and change for the better. The second is the pessimist's choice: Become caught up in what you cannot control, and get stuck in self-pity and a negative outlook that precludes any action:

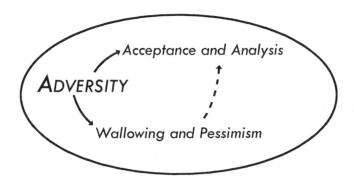

Say you get passed over for a promotion. You can get depressed, call your buddy in another office, and commiserate. You can spend days obsessing and working at half speed. You can entertain negative thoughts to the point of obsession. Or you can employ a positive attitude and rely on the power of "and then some." You can move on to acceptance and the objective analysis of where you had control and where you did not. You can make sure not to lose time on self-pity or worrying about whatever happened that brought about the failure. What's done is done. Your job now is to figure out what's in your power to do to move forward. Further, maintaining a positive attitude will not only benefit you but will inspire others.

There is nothing new here about the importance of positive thinking, but we believe it is crucial to remind people how powerful it is. It's too easy to become lax in applying it. Further, it seems we all have some hidden instinct to find solace in complaining. Even if you naturally have a positive mind-set, there is tremendous temptation to commiserate with others who are caught up in self-pity. Extending compassion to a hurting colleague is one thing, but don't let yourself get caught up in the downward spiral of self-pity and complaining. Think of self-pity as your conscious thought gone awry. It's a disease, and a highly contagious one at that. At first it seems innocuous—who wouldn't feel bad over a lost promotion or a botched presentation?—but if indulged, self-pity becomes incredibly destructive and contributes to lots of lost time and energy. The key to getting past this destructive behavior is accepting responsibility for the part, if any, you played in creating the adversity and then quickly moving on to analyzing objectively what went wrong. From there you need to set a course of action and follow through: Determine what you have control over, what you can change, and then spend all your efforts doing what you can to improve. As for those things you don't have the power to change, externalize them: Don't waste your time feeling bad about things you can't control. Instead, internalize and act upon the things you *can* do to improve your future.

Take, for example, the entrepreneur who had the small fledgling company in good economic times but for whom recession has created dire straits. Focusing on what the company once was and even on the current recession has no value to the entrepreneur. Determining what needs to be done to be successful with the new lay of the land does.

The Process of Self-Improvement

Or consider this real-life example: On one occasion, two colleagues participated in a presentation that received overwhelmingly negative feedback and the eventual loss of a key customer. One of them obsessed for days, worrying not only about an upcoming appraisal, but also about its negative impact on his entire career. Instead of working to improve an obvious weakness, he got stalled out by pessimistic thinking. He got stuck in a downward spiral of pessimism, and his success trajectory took a backward slip. His colleague, on the other hand, immediately inquired further into the feedback and focused not on the failure, but on what could be improved. She received constructive criticism and support from her supervisor that enabled her to go forward. Now, right from the start, which of these workers will not only go on to a more successful life but also a happier one? Those who have traction with optimism and can resist the suction of pessimism and continually get ahead.

We can tell you the end to this particular story, and, unfortunately, it's just what you'd expect. The pessimistic worker was unable to recover from the failure. Instead of taking what he'd learned and moving forward, he got stuck in a downward spiral of self-pity. He hung on for a few months, but eventually ended up leaving his position. His colleague, however, chose to look on her experience of adversity as something like a blessing in disguise (i.e., she made adversity her friend). The negative feedback served as a wake-up call that she needed to hone her preparation and presentation skills. She did, and she delivered an amazing presentation two months later. She remained with the company for nearly a decade and in that time rose to a position of prominence. The discipline of positive and optimistic thought needs to be continually worked and perfected until it is an ingrained habit, as second nature to us as brushing our teeth every morning.

Positive thinking is integral to befriending adversity and to harnessing the power of "and then some." To face adversity and to conduct some honest and effective introspection, you need to have the right frame of mind. Without a positive attitude, you'll just wilt before adversity. Far better is to start with the viewpoint that adversity has something powerful, possibly even life-changing, to teach you.

Now what about those of you who are thinking, "But I'm a pessimist by nature. It's difficult for me to have a positive attitude." Here's our answer: Try it! Just try out a positive mind-set. Face an adversity with a relentlessly positive frame of mind, even if at first it feels artificial or unnatural. After all, the results will be the same regardless of whether or not a positive attitude feels familiar or unfamiliar, authentic or contrived. Allow no other thought to enter your mind than "I will face this adversity head-on and I will learn from it." For the most pessimistic of you, it's going to take a monumental effort, and here's where you can call upon all of your "and then some" resources. Keep at it, and we bet you'll be so impressed with what you learn and with the results you produce that you'll make a habit of positive thinking. And a positive attitude coupled with the power of "and then some" makes for guaranteed human capital development. Before you know it you'll be on the fast track to attaining business savvy and lasting success.

The Age of the Millennials

Let us close this chapter on the power of "and then some" with a special look at the generation just entering the workforce. This group of young people is known as the Millennials. The Millennials are giving many people cause for concern; in fact, they've got some future employers downright nervous.

The funny thing is, this generation should be the most productive ever to enter the American workforce. They don't need secretaries, for their keyboarding skills have them typing faster than they can talk or dictate. They know their way around the Internet and have been raised in an era in which multitasking is the way of the land. They can throw together a slick PowerPoint presentation in minutes that takes older generations days to do. They stay connected twenty-four hours a day, seven days a week. Whether they are e-mailing, text messaging, or doing research over the Net without leaving the bedroom, they are leaps and bounds ahead of prior generations in terms of their efficiency and productivity potential.

In theory, they should also be happier than previous generations. They enjoy innovative technologies and newfound luxuries that are designed to make life easier, quicker, better. They have multiple TV channels, cell phones, BlackBerry smartphones, Treos, Sidekicks, video games, the Internet, iPods, and iPhones. Their houses are larger, their families are smaller, and the average family owns more cars than at any other time in history. Life seems to be easier all around, actually. There are pass/fail classes in which everyone passes and sporting events in which everyone is a winner. At some schools, students who fail to turn in an assignment still get a fifty on a scale of zero to one hundred.

Here is the conundrum: All these kids should be revolutionizing the workforce and producing results never before seen, but this is not happening to the degree one would expect. All these kids, with the unprecedented economic and technological progress they enjoy, should be happier and should be living easier lives. But studies indicate that depression is actually on the rise, especially among young people.

What's going on with the Millennials? Could it be that their terrifically easy lives—or, put another way, their lack of adversity—is exactly the problem?

One striking difference between theirs and older generations is that many Millennials have been raised by affluent parents, parents who are able not only to provide every advantage but also to shelter their kids from adversity, to provide them a safety net for every eventuality. Please don't get us wrong. No one is faulting parents for wanting the best for their children and for being good providers. But we wonder if, in providing everything and preventing their kids from experiencing and working through difficult situations, parents have helped their kids avoid much of the pain and challenges associated with growing up that older generations went through. Learning to overcome adversity and then growing from the experience was perhaps the most important teaching instrument older generations had.

Many people are concerned that Millennials are ill prepared to face the slightest adversity. Job hopping has replaced putting in time with a new employer to work out any frustrations. Younger generations also tend to expect to roll into work dressed casually, have flexible hours, or work from home. They want and even expect to find a work environment that is as forgiving as the environment in which they grew up. Accustomed to such easy and forgiving environments, many members of the younger workforce do not have the cognitive thought process or the skills in place to deal with adversity. We fear that they will learn the hard way that many business opportunities don't have safety nets and not everyone wins. If you miss a meeting or a sales call, you do not get fifty points out of a hundred, you get zero.

In this regard, those who grew up from the humblest of beginnings, without safety nets, may actually have an advantage over those who grew up with everything. Those who grew up disadvantaged tend to develop the power of "and then some" at an early age, many as a survival mechanism. Often, not overcoming adversity was just not an option, and certainly there was little time for self-pity.

The good news for Millennials or for others who have not been personally tried by adversity is that anyone can learn from those who have. We hope that the stories in *The Adversity Paradox* will convince you that adversity need not be the end of the line. Indeed, it is just the beginning.

The Adversity Paradox Takeaways: Making Adversity Your Friend

- Faced with the right attitude, adversity may be the best catalyst for human capital development.
- The simplest understanding of "and then some" is giving the little extra in everything you do. The power of "and then some" can be used to befriend adversity and to become more successful in both your professional and personal life. If you can harness its power, success will become a routine occurrence.
- You have control over your reaction to adversity. You can either wallow in self-pity and pessimism or you can treat adversity as the clarion call to institute needed change.

- Adversity during one's formative years has traditionally been a tremendous teacher, but because of economic progress the role of adversity in shaping us for the future has been diminished. The business world will always be full of adversity, and teaching future business leaders how to learn from adversity and grow their individual human capital is more important than ever before.

4

Just Add Introspection:
Human Capital Component No. 1

Let's face a terribly unfortunate fact of the business world: Most businesses absolutely stink at assisting employee development through formal appraisal processes. It's a major missed opportunity, as we spend such a high percentage of our waking hours at work and good feedback could be so valuable. It's not surprising to hear of people who've never had an appraisal or have one only every couple of years when their boss gets around to it. What's more, even when companies do have a process in place, appraisals can be fraught with subjective and uncorroborated feedback, leaving the employee in a veritable fun house of distorting mirrors, headed in the wrong direction or careening down dead ends.

Business leaders or managers do have good intentions when implementing appraisal processes. They aim to facilitate honest self-assessment so as to maximize employee potential, but more often than not, their execution destroys their intent of growing the human capital within their organizations. When was the last time you heard a manager excited about preparing and delivering an appraisal? When was it anything other than extra work piled on top of an already jam-packed workload? When did you see an appraisal conducted more than just once per year, and without a mentality of "what have you done for me lately?" as opposed to being results-driven and providing sound development suggestions for going forward?

Some businesses do a good job of this admittedly difficult and arduous task, but there are a number of flaws in the standardized appraisal process that hamper its effectiveness from the outset. Many appraisals are based upon subjective one-to-five rating systems for performance issues like quality of work, cooperation and relationships, and problem analysis. They call for one person's subjective opinion, and if your performance issue doesn't show up on the form, tough luck. It's no wonder that even the most skilled and objective of bosses, faced with these off-the-shelf, one-size-fits-all appraisal forms, can find it difficult to do a good job of employee assessment. Then there are the not-so-unusual cases where a change in supervisor produces a large change in a person's appraisal score—no change in performance, mind you, just a change in who's doing the appraising. More often than not, these situations are caused by a weak manager giving years of glowing appraisals for mediocre (or worse) work in an effort to avoid potentially disenfranchising a subordinate. After all, a manager's job is to motivate, not undermine. These types of failures are typical, and they're true testimony to how appraisal systems have the capability to provide distorted mirrors.

So far we're probably not telling you anything new, right? But it's important to get to the next step, which is recognizing that there is no substitute for real introspection, for an honest and critical examination of one's own thoughts, feelings, and motivations, and by extension, one's strengths and weaknesses. With the process of introspection, one takes in all the reflections that multiple mirrors provide and synthesizes them into a true image. In other words, introspection offers an accurate personal appraisal process that enables one to analyze motives and priorities and to measure progress and commitments toward goals. The business-savvy professional must take responsibility for setting up his or her own mirrors, accepting and understanding their reflections, and making whatever adjustments are needed when mirrors reveal a weakness. The process of introspection allows one to make constant—and accurate—trajectory adjustments.

We found that those who have reached the upper levels of success not only are skilled at introspection but also have flawless mirrors. They really know who they are, recognize what they do well and what they've done to contribute to their successes, and see needs for improvement and what they've done to contribute to their failures; and they never wait for someone else to step forward and provide them with an appraisal. Instead, they are proactive in finding ways to bombard themselves with mirrors that give true reflections, and then they digest those reflections into accurate introspection. Their ability to continually make trajectory corrections is essential to building their human capital and thus their business savvy.

Critical to successful introspection is that it is conducted with *frequency* and with *accuracy*. Frequent but inaccurate introspection gets one nowhere and can even be self-destructive—we've all seen people who exaggerated their weaknesses and needlessly beat themselves down into a state of learned helplessness in which they erroneously believed that they had no control over a situation and that their actions were futile. Accurate but infrequent introspection just places a person on a low trajectory, as trajectory corrections don't occur often enough.

We need to make introspection as scientific a process as possible, using objective principles for reflection and using critical thinking in analyzing our reflections.

Global Positioning System (GPS)

In 1983 Korean Air Lines flight 007 lost its position in the skies and strayed off course into restricted Russian airspace. Soviet military interceptor jets shot down the aircraft, killing all 269 people on board. It was a terrible human disaster that no one was interested in repeating. In response, President Ronald Reagan announced that a new global positioning system, designed and built by the United States, would be made available for civilian uses. This system, commonly referred to as GPS, came online in 1993. It is made up of more than two dozen satellites orbiting the earth that transmit signals. Through triangulation, anyone with a GPS receiver can use these signals to determine a fix on their location, speed, and direction. Today the use of the GPS has exploded beyond the airline industry. It's an increasingly common navigational aid in cars, and it's also used for boat navigation, with heavy equipment for construction, on bicycles for racing and touring, by hikers, for Google maps, and even on the golf course.

Triangulation is simply the use of a mathematical equation. The satellites transmit signals. GPS receivers pick up these signals when they have an unobstructed view of a satellite. Each signal includes information on the location of the satellite and the time the signal was sent. The signals travel at a known speed. Satellites and receivers both contain clocks. Receivers are able to calculate the distance to a satellite by measuring the time delay between when a signal was sent and when it was received. Obtaining the signal from one satellite does not provide enough mathematical information to provide a fix on a location. But when a receiver can determine the position of and distance to additional satellites, it has enough information to compute its position. A GPS receiver's accuracy is highly dependent on its clock synchronizing with the satellite system. This is accomplished by picking up and comparing signals with additional satellites.

There are two critical things the GPS points out to us as we strive to build and maximize our business savvy and improve our introspection skills. First, just as a GPS receiver provides accurate information only when multiple signals are picked up, so is a person's introspection accuracy improved with multiple mirrors. The greater the number of mirrors, the more likely we are to gain an accurate reading of our location, speed, and direction. Second, we have to be able to triangulate those reflections as a GPS receiver does—in other words, synthesize the data coming to us from our multiple mirrors—in order to get an accurate reading of where and who we are, the speed we are moving, and the direction we are going. It is crucial to maintaining and improving trajectory.

Satellites and Mirrors

When we were young we were surrounded by mirrors that told us what we were doing right, what we were doing wrong, and what we could do differently—we usually had far more mirrors than we appreciated! Parents, teachers, test scores, report cards, coaches, counselors, sports successes and failures, and even things such as piano recitals were all there to give us rapid feedback. In those days we didn't have to ask for or seek out mirrors for reflection, either written or verbal. Each ball game helped tell us what sort of athlete we were; each test score told us exactly how we were doing academically; awards or teacher feedback told us whether we were excelling at piano, poetry, or painting. Frequency was clearly not a problem, and with so many focused and often objective mirrors we could get a pretty accurate read on who we were and in what areas we might be able to excel.

But then sometimes mirrors seem to provide conflicting reflections, and this is exactly where triangulation comes in. Take Ben Carson, for example, today one of the most recognized brain surgeons in the world. At thirteen he was failing in school. His poor grades might have been an accurate reflection of his efforts, but his mother functioned as another mirror. She knew he had potential, and to help him realize it, she made him check out two books from the Detroit Public Library and write book reports on them each week. She even went so far as to grade his reports, making check marks and highlights. Carson didn't discover for years that his mother's marks were a ruse; she had only a third-grade education and was illiterate. But she did know that the people whose houses she cleaned spent more time reading books than watching TV, and those book reports helped to spark an unquenchable thirst for knowledge in Carson. Eventually, his grades soared. He went on to earn a scholarship to Yale University and at thirty-two, became the youngest chief of pediatric neurosurgery in Johns Hopkins Hospital's history. Triangulation changed his trajectory, for life.

Peter Dawkins, retired vice chairman of Citigroup Private Bank, who in junior high was struggling in school, transferred and promptly flunked his first semester in a new school. The school was one mirror, his family's belief in him another, and the experience of successfully combating polio as a child was a third. Through triangulation Dawkins was able to synthesize all the reflections coming to him—failure in school, a fresh chance at school, his family's belief in him, firsthand experience that adversity could be overcome—and his life changed for the better. Left without mirrors, there's no telling where Carson or Dawkins would be today.

As we age, many of our mirrors disappear. No grades, coaches, music recitals, or parents. Certainly some mirrors are replaced—perhaps with a spouse, boss, or friends—but the average person is left with far fewer means to obtain accurate and frequent reflections. It's only natural that one can easily lose his or her fix on location, speed, and direction in the less structured adult environment, producing the potential for plateauing a trajectory or even falling from it. Just as the key to the GPS is having multiple satellites and accurate signals at all times, the key to good introspection is having multiple mirrors and accurate reflections at all times. In both cases, one needs to be able to triangulate.

Harvey Mackay, successful business owner, Horatio Alger member, and author of several bestselling books, including *Swim with the Sharks Without Being Eaten Alive,* may demonstrate the value of multiple mirrors best. To this day he relies on what he calls eighteen coaches—everyone from marathon, writing, and language and speech coaches to a humor coach. He learned the value of multiple mirrors early when he bought his struggling company. He was twenty-six, and back then he called each of his mirrors "old grizzly," as his lawyer was sixty, his accountant fifty-eight, and his banker somewhere north of seventy. His was a professional team, but mirrors need not cost money. "There are a lot of qualified advisors out there," Mackay said, "who are just waiting for us to ask them. Try it sometime." He also emphasizes that "you may have to listen more than you talk, but that won't hurt you, either." Clearly, the success of Harvey Mackay has been impacted by the many mirrors he has been proactive about establishing. His success has little to do with luck and everything to do with the science of setting up mirrors (satellites) and conducting accurate and frequent introspection (triangulation).

The Mackay approach stands in stark contrast to many in business today. Take the competent businessperson who relies solely on his boss or his appraisal as his performance and trajectory gauge. As a GPS receiver cannot provide an accurate fix on location with a single satellite, neither can the businessperson conduct accurate introspection with only one mirror. Now, who has the better chance of continually making accurate adjustments to their trajectory and building their business savvy to its fullest potential: the Harvey Mackays of the world or the businessperson with one mirror?

Lee Liu

Lee Liu knows himself as well as anyone. He credits accurate and frequent introspection as being the most significant factor in helping him overcome great odds to rise to a position of leadership as a CEO.

Not only did Liu came from humble beginnings, but also his life's circumstances provided little or no opportunity even to establish a trajectory before entering college. Liu was born in China in 1933 just prior to the conflict with Japan in 1937. With his father serving in the Chinese military, the rest of his family fled for the safety of southern China to avoid the invading Japanese. After the war his family reunited for a short time before civil war broke out, but as that war advanced they were forced to move to safety in Hong Kong. After two years and after having their properties confiscated by the Communists, the family scraped together what they could and emigrated to Brazil.

By this time, Liu was sixteen. His life had been spent fleeing wars and he had attended school only sporadically. He had seen his parents lose not only their personal wealth, but also their culture and their social status. Liu's father had been a high-ranking general in the Chinese army and later the governor of the province of Fujian. Despite the upheaval and adversities for Liu and his six siblings, his parents somehow maintained a positive and influential attitude. Liu recalls often hearing his father say, "Get educated and make yourself useful." For Liu, being able to carry on this positive attitude for years to come would help lead him to develop the perseverance it took to succeed.

If the readjustment to Hong Kong and its brand-new surroundings was difficult, the readjustment to Brazil was grueling. There Liu encountered new surroundings, a new culture, a new government, and a new language. His father bought into a rock quarry and a coffee plantation with what money they had left and tried to make a go of it. Having been a civil servant all his life and having no experience in business or farming, Liu's father struggled. To help out, Liu dropped out of school and drove a truck for the business. He found that he was intrigued by the business and he wanted to learn all he could about it.

Eventually he returned to school and decided to pursue a higher education as his father had wished. Being resourceful, he went through an American Information Services office in Brazil and applied to several U.S. universities; he was accepted at Iowa State University in Ames, Iowa. Just getting to school involved two weeks on a boat and then trains and buses. This move would create new insights into what Liu wanted to do with his future. "When I came to the United States," he said, "I saw everyone working, from the paperboy to the milkman. Everyone was making a contribution to society and I knew this is where I wanted to stay."

In school he had limited financial resources. He worked more than thirty hours a week to cover tuition and room and board. His jobs included busing tables, cleaning dorms, assisting a professor, painting student housing, and manually setting pins at a university bowling alley. Despite all this, it took Liu just a little over three years to graduate with a bachelor's degree in electrical engineering.

After college Liu planned to spend three more years in the United States gaining experience and then return to Brazil. He joined Iowa Electric, a utility company, not realizing he would become passionate about his work. "I had the satisfaction of restoring power to whole neighborhoods when there were blackouts," he said. "I worked long hours in Iowa's rural areas, driving all over restoring service. After one storm I worked thirty-three hours straight. When I turned on a switch and lights came on for hundreds of families, it made me feel good." Iowa Electric, later renamed Alliant Energy, ended up being a lifelong career for Liu.

Most people would fold against the odds Liu faced. What makes the Lee Lius of this world different?

The Liu GPS

Lee Liu was able to internalize an attitude of perseverance, whereas most persons under similar circumstances are in danger of adopting learned helplessness and failure. In his story we see a lot of similarities with others who have succeeded after having such a humble start in life. Despite his sporadic early education Liu saw needs for knowledge and looked to satisfy them. His story also demonstrates that very few resources are needed to build a personal GPS. All one needs is the ability to find mirrors in new environments and use them. Constantly being uprooted and being forced to adapt to new environments contributed to Liu's GPS-building ability and certainly to his later ability to build business savvy.

"The first sixteen years of my life were spent constantly fleeing and staying ahead of wars," he said. "I witnessed the horrors of war while my family traveled with all the food, water, and fuel we could carry, slept in the car from time to time, and took refuge wherever possible. There were some brief periods of stability, but more often than not I was in a new and different environment." As a young kid, Liu had to figure out who he was in each new village, town, or city.

After the move to Brazil, Liu realized that returning to his homeland and culture was not possible. This was overwhelming for a sixteen-year-old, but Liu would later reflect on it as being a blessing in disguise. Closing the door on the past just meant he would be more aggressive in figuring out the future, a new culture and new language. "I didn't know it at the time, but I was gaining introspection skills," he said. "With each new move I started to better understand how I could fit in and make the best of my surroundings." Frequent introspection became a necessity for surviving in new environments. Just a couple of years in Brazil were enough for him to learn Portuguese and get enough mirrors established to start envisioning his future. Some of those mirrors reflected the fact that he was smart enough to go to college. Another mirror was a family from Illinois that he befriended in Brazil; they would be influential in his going to the United States to go to school. With these mirrors, plus the mirror his father's business provided, Liu had the means for triangulation.

When he arrived in the United States he was only eighteen and looking to adapt to his third culture, language, and political system. That adjustment could be a recipe for disaster for many, but because of the skills he'd gained in overcoming adversity, Liu saw it as an opportunity. "I recognized at the time that I was a minority and first-generation immigrant and I would have to work harder and smarter than others to be successful," Liu said. This is remarkably accurate introspection for such a young person.

His skill at introspection didn't mean the transition would be easy. The States and school were a real struggle for Liu at first. "When I came to college I thought I knew everything, and college was a rude awakening," he said. "I recognized I knew very little and I quickly figured out I was starting from scratch." A young person thinking that he knows everything is not unusual, but recognizing such fallacious thinking while still young is. The school was yet another mirror, and Liu was quickly able to make some trajectory adjustments; primarily, he had to work extra hard to succeed academically.

With prior moves he at least had a few mirrors available in his parents and siblings. In the United States he had to go to work building a new GPS. Over time he accumulated more mirrors— grades, friends, professors, his Brazilian wife whom he met while at school, and the college dean. After college he would add his coworkers and his church. He describes his improvements to reflect and triangulate over the years as being a direct result not only of adding mirrors but also of increasing his sensitivity to them. "In my career, when I had a failure, I learned to look at the goals I had set out and what my reflections were telling me, recalibrate and move forward."

Liu's story proves that a personal GPS can be established quickly when needed. In his case, he got good at introspection when he was young. His quick establishment of a new GPS in every new environment, and his continuing use of introspection, were critical to making him successful.

Doris Christopher

At the age of thirty-five, a mother and homemaker borrowed $3,000 against her husband's life insurance policy and started a business in her basement. That business is now a household name, has grown to more than $700 million in sales, and has more than 1,000 direct employees, 70,000 indirect employees, and 12 million customers. That woman is Doris Christopher, and her business is the Pampered Chef.

Christopher grew up on the outskirts of Chicago and was the youngest of three girls. Her father was a self-employed businessman who owned and operated his own one-man gas station. He worked six days a week, ten hours a day, and covered all aspects of the business, from pumping gas to being a top-notch mechanic. Christopher's mother also worked, so it was always a busy household, but the family was very close. "Weekends seemed very special, especially Sundays," Christopher said. "We spent the entire day together as a family. We went to church, had dinner together, and watched *The Ed Sullivan Show* on TV." Christopher went on to graduate from the University of Illinois at Champaign with a bachelor's degree in home economics. She then taught that subject for six years before becoming a stay-at-home mom until her daughters entered school.

With the cost of college for her two daughters looming, she decided to go back to work to supplement the family income. At first she dabbled with some part-time work—teaching sewing at Montgomery Ward, doing alterations, testing cake mixes, and finally demonstrating Jenn-Air ranges. While she enjoyed these things, they were not the ideal jobs for balancing family and work, and she committed herself to finding something she could do on her own terms that would not take away from her family.

Knowing that she was outstanding in the kitchen, she struck upon a business premise that would cater to her strengths and interests. She would search out and buy unique, top-quality kitchen utensils wholesale, personally demonstrate them in home kitchen shows, and sell them. With the support and help of her husband, Christopher launched the business and took herself along the learning curve, teaching herself everything from purchasing, inventory management, hiring, and facilities—in short, everything involved with running and growing a business. The results speak to her success. Warren Buffett may have stated it best: "I would challenge anyone on Wall Street to take

$3,000 and do what Doris Christopher has done: build a busi-
ness from scratch into a world-class organization."

The Christopher GPS

Christopher displays all the human capital components of the
business-savvy professional. She has a strong value system to guide
her and the Pampered Chef, the roots of which can be seen from
her childhood days with her parents. She found a purpose that she
became very passionate about: making family mealtime special
and being involved in work that would help bring families together.
She demonstrated a strong work character in getting the Pampered
Chef off the ground while keeping up with her responsibilities as a
mother and a wife and adding the skills she needed to run a large
and successful business. Christopher was always filling knowledge
voids as she and her coworkers ventured into unknown territories.

Doris Christopher's recognition as a Horatio Alger member
came not so much for her humble beginnings as a child, but for
her humble business beginnings. You can't grow a business as
fast and as big as she did without having a great personal GPS
system. How does one do it starting at age thirty-five, and without the necessary skill set?

Critical to her start-up and growing of the business was the
mentoring she received from her husband, Jay. Christopher
refers to him as her loving husband while he refers to himself as
her "mentor and tormentor." "Jay is a masterful devil's advocate,"
she said. "He's always confronting me to look for the less-than-
obvious solutions. Like a therapist, he asks pointed questions that
make me think—and come up with my own answers." Before
starting the business he got Christopher to sit down and list all
her skills and the things she liked to do. Then he had her list all

the jobs that might incorporate those things along with the advantages and disadvantages of each. Later, with the business in a critical phase of trying to get off the ground, Christopher scheduled and then canceled her first kitchen show out of fear of public speaking. Jay was the one who would not let her back down from the rescheduled show, and as it turned out, she loved it. She couldn't have asked for a better mirror.

Christopher was also keen to continue adding mirrors as she grew the business. They included everyone from her customers to her employees, from her suppliers to her kitchen consultants. Having started on the ground floor herself, working directly with customers and employees, she has always been able to relate well to any kind of employee.

Before the business outgrew her house, she would have all her kitchen consultants over each month and gather reflections on how they were doing, what products were selling and why, and what they could do better. Triangulating the reflections of her husband, customers, coworkers, and kitchen consultants allowed her to constantly adjust her trajectory upward.

She also discovered how mirrors can wear out, be outgrown, or just need adjustment from time to time. The initial growth of the Pampered Chef was largely due to Christopher's involvement on the front lines doing kitchen shows or working directly with her kitchen consultants, getting feedback on what worked and what did not. But as the number of kitchen consultants grew Christopher found herself in the somewhat enviable position of having too many mirrors.

Knowing that reflections from the consultants were what made the company thrive, the Pampered Chef put in place a process to provide clearer reflections and to synthesize them. Committees of kitchen consultants were established. Although unpaid, being a committee member has become a highly sought-after position. Committee members are selected from all levels of the kitchen consultant organization so as to provide a cross section. The committees have successfully replaced the early mirrors of individual kitchen consultants and now serve to provide the means for the invaluable asset of accurate and frequent introspection.

Mentors

Mentors of all types are extremely important for increasing both the accuracy and the frequency of your introspection. The term "mentor" can apply to any person who is offering you feedback for forward thinking and positive adjustments. The more mentors, the better the triangulation, and more often than not, mentoring is free for the asking.

Ron Willingham, the founder of Integrity Systems, knows well the value of mentoring. He grew up living with his mother, father, and two sisters in a four-room house on the outskirts of a small Texas oil town. His bedroom was the tiny kitchen, where they would push the dinette aside at night and open up his narrow rollaway bed. Early mentors inspired him to think beyond what appeared to be limitations and to dream of starting his own company. That dream would eventually be realized in Integrity Systems.

Since Willingham founded his organization in the 1960s, more than two million people in sixty-five countries have taken his courses. His flagship product and course is Integrity Selling.

Willingham is the architect of Integrity Selling, and through it he has developed an incredible understanding of how the human mind works. As someone who was mentored and then became very successful at mentoring others, he has great insight. He offered these comments when asked about finding mentors:

> Find people who are achieving the level of success that you'd like to enjoy, and learn from them. One might ask why a highly successful person would want to spend time with them. What I have learned about highly successful people is they have a strong need to perpetuate their success, so they're quite willing to share ideas with people who sincerely want to learn from them. In addition, most highly successful people owe their beginning to one or two other high achievers who mentored them. Helping others is a way of paying back the people who helped them on their way up. There have been several high achievers whom I have asked to learn from, including Dr. Maxwell Maltz, author of *Psycho-Cybernetics,* who spent many hours with me over the years. I consider the courses I have developed and the books I have written as a way of paying him and my other mentors back.

Willingham points out that successful people want to give back. They are often flattered when asked to be a mentor.

Mirrors Don't Always Offer Reflections We Like

Many reflections, along with the subsequent introspection that must follow, are actually very uncomfortable. Barry was in direct insurance sales early in his career. Sales is a difficult profession for those who struggle with rejection—there is no profession with more mirrors. You have daily sales calls, most of which don't result in a sale, a manager, sales associates, all with different degrees of success, and normally you have commission-based compensation. People who excel in sales are those who can triangulate these multiple reflections and make trajectory corrections accordingly. Those who cannot handle mirrors reflecting rejection or who cannot triangulate those rejections into trajectory corrections fail quickly.

"Those early days making sales calls were difficult," Barry said. "Dealing with rejection was one thing, turning those rejections into positive adjustments was entirely another. It often took a lot of rejections before I could get an accurate read on exactly what I was doing wrong and what I was doing right."

Rejection never gets easier, although some in sales claim you grow callous. Barry disagrees. "I do not think you grow callous to rejection as you risk losing your sensitivity, which is so important when conducting introspection. What the successful do is gain perseverance so they can both handle rejection and be sensitive to the reflections that can arise."

Hindsight Can Be a Twenty-Twenty Mirror

No one likes to dwell on mistakes, but good businesses take advantage of their pasts, *especially* their failures. Barry uses what his company calls the "Look Back." He described the importance of the Look Back meetings with their Australian losses: "We learned many valuable lessons that, although very costly, made us a much stronger company. Our critical inspection of ourselves has greatly reduced the risks of repeating our mistakes with acquisitions." One issue uncovered was a clash of corporate cultures. The Principal didn't take into account the complexities of converting such a large corporation into their own corporate culture. The Look Back also revealed a hard lesson about respecting the size of acquisitions and allocation of resources to get operations merged. They concluded that they did not move quickly enough to put people in key positions and that they underestimated the amount of transition work necessary and the subsequent timeline for doing it.

With Bob, the process was called the "Postmortem" and was done on construction projects, both winners and losers. It involved bringing together the engineer, architect, builder, key subcontractors, and key suppliers. Everyone wanted to know what went right and what went wrong so that going forward they could be the best that they could be. Whether it was the Look Back or the Postmortem there was a consistent theme: Hindsight was absolutely crucial, and more was learned from failures than from successes. It's the adversity paradox in action.

With individuals, the same program has to apply. This is not to be confused with those who live in the past. This is all about those people who can understand the past and use it as a twenty-twenty mirror so as not to repeat mistakes and to leverage their prior successes.

The Diagnostic Skill of Introspection

Few are born with a gift for introspection. Introspection is a difficult process, and sometimes we flat out don't like what we see and avoid turning reflections into introspection. But great introspection is required of those who want to attain business savvy and be successful, and anyone can learn how to conduct better introspection. It starts by being honest with oneself and understanding honesty's importance for trajectory adjustments. False or errant reflections don't help us move forward and may even harm our trajectories. This is why those with lots of business savvy continually strive to find ways to improve accuracy and frequency. They are always looking to add accurate reflecting mirrors, and they repair or discard old or faulty mirrors. Over time they increase their sensitivity to mirrors, and they conduct introspection with enough frequency that they can maintain a constant upward trajectory.

The Adversity Paradox Takeaways:
A Gut Check on Your GPS

- List the number of orbiting satellites you have acting as mirrors. They could include family members, friends, coworkers, supervisors, and so on. Depending on your aspirations and goals there may also be many more objective mirrors, such as income level, awards, and positions achieved.
- Rank your mirrors on effectiveness. Which ones are providing the most accurate information that you can use for triangulation? Are there any that are ineffective to the point they need to be discarded?
- Determine how you can improve your GPS. Maybe a major overhaul is in order, or maybe just a few satellites need to be upgraded or tuned up. And never hesitate to add satellites. The more you have, the more accurate your introspection should be for providing a read on your location, speed, and direction in the journey toward attaining your goals.

5

What Does Behavior Have to Do with Values? Everything!
Human Capital Component No. 2

Possessing business savvy isn't just about superior business skills or proficiency in a particular area of business. It's also about having the right values and bringing those values to bear on the way one does business.

Unfortunately, we live in a time that may very well go down in history as the era of corporate greed and moral ineptitude. For a while the news has been saturated with stories of fraud, underreporting, overcharging, bribery, theft, insider dealing, and abuses of privilege. Fresh in our minds is the long list of casualties from the subprime fiasco, including the government takeover of "Freddie and Fannie," and an unprecedented amount spent by governments around the world to rescue financial institutions. Before that were the large-scale travails at companies such as Enron, WorldCom, Tyco, and HealthSouth. Others may remember the savings and loan collapse of the mid-1980s—and the $125 billion tab that taxpayers subsequently picked up. The stars on this dubious stage are the business leaders who will be remembered not for their business savvy or their extraordinary success, but for massive ethical failure. This all rings of history repeating itself.

In 1999, Charles Keating, who headed Lincoln Savings and Loan of Irvine, California, admitted in a plea agreement to four counts of fraud and taking money from American Continental Corporation, parent company of Lincoln, all while he knew the S&L would collapse within weeks.

Michael Milken, perhaps better known as the "Junk Bond King," was charged by Rudy Giuliani, then a United States attorney, with ninety-nine counts of racketeering and fraud. He pleaded guilty to six lesser securities violations relating to insider trading and tax fraud.

Former Tyco International CEO Dennis Kozlowski and former Tyco CFO Mark H. Swartz were both convicted on charges of theft for personal gain. Kowolski and Swartz were accused of stealing more than $600 million from the company. Both were sentenced to jail and ordered to pay hefty restitution fines.

An $11 billion accounting scandal contributed to the bankruptcy of WorldCom, up until then the second-largest long-distance phone company in the United States. The company emerged from bankruptcy in 2004, but in 2005 their former CEO Bernard Ebbers was convicted of fraud and conspiracy.

Enron, of course, has been one of the most publicized corporate scandals. The company had 21,000 employees at the time of its collapse. Top executive abuses ran the gamut from accounting fraud to theft. The scandal also brought down the accounting firm of Arthur Andersen.

As the past is the best predictor of the future, we can only assume the financial crisis triggered by subprime lending practices will produce an even larger list of bad characters.

Some notable common themes emerge from these debacles. In all these cases, those participitating in the fraud paid a price that included humiliation, legal fines, ruined careers, and often, jail time. Each one involved the top executives. Each necessitated coconspirators who worked for those top executives. Each involved falsifying financials. But what's most glaring is that each CEO placed his monetary well-being and his ego above everyone else. There were no legitimate legal or character defenses of "I needed to do it to protect my employees" or "It was in the best interest of our stockholders." These people were motivated by sheer self-interest; they were out to protect themselves and their kingdoms. They were looking out for one person and one person only, and in the end, everyone lost.

Interestingly, it's safe to say that most if not all of the executives perpetuating these crimes actually had plenty of business savvy—there's no doubt they were some of the most capable and knowledgeable business people around. But their fatal flaw—a lack of moral development—brought down their businesses, destroyed their credibility, and did incalculable damage to their employees, their stockholders, their families, their customers, and certainly, themselves.

If there was any good to come from this rampant moral failure, it was that widespread corrective actions began taking place. Business ethics classes are now de rigueur for MBAs. Many businesses distribute codes of conduct or codes of ethics and have employees sign off on them annually. Others conduct in-house ethics classes.

But while ethical companies do employ these very necessary measures, even the most carefully thought-out and well-executed plans to encourage ethical behavior fail from time to time. We must remember that simply signing off on a piece of paper doesn't ensure ethical behavior. Enron's sixty-four-page code of ethics has been widely publicized. The last known edition was published in July 2000, while leadership was actively engaged in fraud. It's yet another case of the disconnect that can occur between a company's stated values and its actual behavior. A company's true values are what they express with their behaviors.

As the savings and loan crisis brought about new regulations, and debacles such as Enron gave us Sarbanes-Oxley, we can anticipate another set of rules and regulations devised to avoid another major financial crisis. Certainly some legislation is needed, but does more regulation really address the root cause of such nightmares? More than 2,000 years ago, Plato said, "Good people do not need laws to tell them to act responsibly, while bad people will find a way around the laws."

We believe any measures businesses take to encourage ethical behavior in their employees is certainly a step in the right direction. Creating and fostering a culture of integrity and ethical behavior is not only the right thing to do, it's critical to business success. It should get the same kind of attention as customer focus, operational excellence, employee development, and superior performance for shareholders. The culture of integrity and ethical behavior must start at the top, too. Leaders need to set and live out the example for their organizations, and it's all too obvious how one corrupt manager can bring down an entire company. It is extremely difficult for employees to develop morally under corrupt leaders.

At the end of the day, the most effective tool anyone has is his or her own behavior, and behavior is always ultimately predicated upon an individual choice. So now we'd like to narrow our focus from the corporate to the individual and spend some time examining the basis of ethical behavior, individual moral reasoning.

Kohlbergian Theory

Lawrence Kohlberg was a psychologist and professor at the University of Chicago and Harvard University. His research holds that moral reasoning, which is the basis for ethical behavior, has six identifiable developmental stages. To develop his theory Kohlberg created the Moral Development Interview. Subjects were presented with ethical dilemmas that required them to use moral reasoning to come to a conclusion. The results of the recorded interviews were scored according to the justification subjects made as to why they considered certain actions right or wrong. A typical fictitious moral dilemma Kohlberg used is called "Heinz Steals the Drug in Europe":

> In Europe, a woman was near death from a very bad disease, a special kind of cancer. There was one drug that the doctors thought might save her. It was a form of radium that a druggist in the same town had recently discovered. The drug was expensive to make, but the druggist was charging ten times what the drug cost him to produce. He paid $200 for the radium and charged $2,000 for a small dose of the drug. The sick woman's husband, Heinz, went to everyone he knew to borrow the money, but he could get together only about $1,000, which was half of what it cost. He told the druggist that his wife was dying and asked him to sell it cheaper or let him pay later. But the druggist said, "No, I discovered the drug and I'm going to

make money from it." Heinz got desperate and broke into the man's store to steal the drug for his wife.

Should the husband have done that? Was it right or wrong?

Based upon people's motivations for the course of action they chose, Kohlberg developed three levels and six stages of moral development:

Level	Stage	Characteristics of Stage and Level
Preconventional	1	Punishment-obedience
	2	Self-interest
Conventional	3	Interpersonal accord and conformity
	4	Authority and social order
Postconventional	5	Social contract
	6	Universal ethical principles

Level I: Preconventional Morality

This level should be the easiest for all of us to understand, as we were all there once, probably in preadolescence. Stage 1 is simply the rules and punishment trade-off. Thinkers using stage 1 moral reasoning believe that there is an external and fixed set of rules, and that there is only one right or wrong answer to every moral dilemma. As there is only one right choice, stage 1 thinkers would avoid making the "wrong" choice in order to escape punishment. If Heinz were using stage 1 reasoning, he would not steal the drug simply because he wants to avoid prison. In the work environment, an employee would refrain from unethical behavior to avoid being written up, demoted, or fired.

In stage 2 of the preconventional level, individuals lock into a "what's in it for me" perspective. All behavior comes from serving one's own needs. A person at this stage can see from the perspective of others but only from the standpoint of gaining some reciprocity: I'll scratch your back if you scratch mine. Using stage 2 reasoning, Heinz would steal the drug because he would be much happier if he saves his wife. In the work environment, one may expend extra effort only in order to get a raise.

Level II: Conventional Morality

Those in stage 3 base moral choices on the expectations of others in their proximity, such as family, friends, peers, and the community. Likewise in business, an employee bases his or her behavior upon the expectations of superiors, coworkers, and subordinates. Stage 3 is sometimes referred to as the "good boy, good girl" stage: People base their choices on a desire to live up to societal expectations. At this third stage of moral reasoning, Heinz would steal the medicine because he wants to be a good husband. Stage 3 business employees would refrain from stealing from the supply room because they don't want to risk others' disapproval. It is possible, however, that if one's social or business milieu is ethically unsound, one would act unethically in order to gain the approval of others and—within this environment—be deemed "good." In the case of Enron, for example, surely some subordinates failed morally in order to gain the approval of their corrupt leaders, or they may have attempted to justify their actions by saying other leaders were doing the same thing.

Stage 4, however, brings us into all new territory. Individuals at this stage have expanded their circle of thinking enough to see the society or the business they are in as a whole. The emphasis is on obeying laws or rules, respecting authority, and handling one's duties so that the social order or business rules and processes are maintained. Though Heinz may steal the drug for his wife based on wholly good intentions, his actual act of theft is wrong. He would acquiesce to the prescribed punishment for the crime. He understands that actions have consequences, and he is willing to accept those consequences. In our business model this is a crucial stage for getting everyone pulling in the same direction. Individuals see themselves as full-fledged team members, vital parts of the whole. If they see things with which they do not agree, they work through business processes to create change. For a business to thrive, employees need to advance to stage 4 at least.

Level III: Postconventional Morality

At the postconventional level people step back and take an even broader view. Empathy not only grows deeper but also expands to include more people and a greater diversity of viewpoints. Stage 5 thinkers want to do what is best for society or for all parties that touch the business. At stage 5, Heinz would steal the medicine because everyone has a right to choose life, regardless of the law. Conversely, he would not steal the medicine because the scientist who made it has a right to fair compensation. Johnson & Johnson CEO James Burke gives a memorable example of stage 5 moral reasoning. Many may remember the Tylenol scare in the 1980s. Pulling the tainted product from the shelves came at tremendous cost to stockholders and risked employee jobs, but Burke knew that it ensured a greater good to society. His decision is remembered as a great ethical decision, and today Johnson & Johnson is recognized as having one of the best corporate reputations in the world.

It is crucial for those in a leadership role to reach this level. At stage 5 one must not only be driven by principle but also understand and balance the interests of everyone. This includes employees, stockholders, customers, their communities, and, increasingly, the environment. Employees need an enormous amount of business experience and institutional knowledge to operate at this level.

Few people reach the level of stage 6 moral reasoning, but those with prodigious business savvy always strive for it. This is the stage of universal human ethics. Behavior is predicated upon actions and decisions that demonstrate an equal respect for all. In this case, Heinz would steal the medicine because saving a human life is a more fundamental value than the property rights of another person, or he would not steal the medicine because others may need it just as badly and their lives are equally significant. This is a stage of radical impartiality; it's the territory of moral exemplars like Mahatma Gandhi and Dr. Martin Luther King Jr. It's difficult if not impossible to reason consistently at this stage; recognizing this, Kohlberg eventually came to view it as a theoretical stage.

Kohlbergian Theory Applied
to the Business Environment

For the long-term growth and health of any business it is crucial to hire ethically sound people and to foster an environment in which employees can develop morally and only the ethically sound are rewarded. Using Kohlberg's theory on moral development we have formulated the hierarchy of moral development in business, a tool that can be easily used to see how far along your own moral development has come and how far you need to go.

Hierarchy of Moral Development in Business

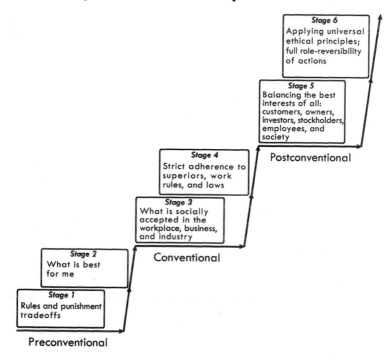

Stage 6
Applying universal ethical principles; full role-reversibility of actions

Stage 5
Balancing the best interests of all: customers, owners, investors, stockholders, employees, and society

Stage 4
Strict adherence to superiors, work rules, and laws

Postconventional

Stage 3
What is socially accepted in the workplace, business, and industry

Stage 2
What is best for me

Conventional

Stage 1
Rules and punishment tradeoffs

Preconventional

Are you a "people pleaser," motivated mainly by a desire to gain the approval of supervisors? Then you're at stage 3—you'll have lots of company there. Or, as a small part of a larger whole, do you act in such a way to ensure the smooth operation of the entire business? If so, you're at stage 4. Are your actions and decisions based upon what would achieve the greater good—even if it flies in the face of company policy or standard operating procedure? If so you're at stage 5.

So how does one climb the hierarchy of moral development, advancing from one stage to the next? What causes a stage 2 thinker who is blinded by self-interest to advance to stage 3, where he or she can at least consider the viewpoint of others? Ethics classes and workshops are wonderful, and we highly recommend them. We feel the same way about written and verbal policies that promote ethical behavior. But case studies, hypothetical situations, and words on paper will take one only so far. In the end we agree with Kohlberg: One advances in moral reasoning by actually encountering a moral dilemma, finding that one's current level of moral reasoning is inadequate, and then grappling with that dilemma to the point that one comes to a more comprehensive viewpoint. In other words, we face a real moral dilemma, discover that our current level of thinking has shortcomings or limitations, and are then forced to come up with a broader, deeper level of moral reasoning. The more comprehensive our viewpoint, the more robust our moral development, and the further we advance up the hierarchy of moral development.

We'd like to suggest that business offers one of the best environments for advancing in moral development. The fact is, people in business routinely face moral dilemmas (surely an exercise in adversity itself!), and as we've seen, it's in working through dilemmas, through being challenged to grow, that we make our way up the hierarchy of moral development.

This does not mean, of course, that you need to experience the likes of the Enrons of the world to gain the experiential learning necessary to climb to new stages of moral development. In fact, we hope you find yourself at a business that's owned and operated by morally sound people, and it goes without saying that we hope you count yourself among them. If your superiors or colleagues are further along the hierarchy of moral development than you are, count yourself lucky: You can learn from their excellent examples and pave the way for your own climb up the hierarchy.

And take care that when you are determining your, or a superior's, position on the hierarchy of moral development that you consider the whole person. We've known people who argued that they can be moral people at home but consider work an entirely different story. We've seen the converse, too: people who claim to practice exemplary business ethics but whose behavior outside of work is downright shocking. Neither of these scenarios makes sense. You do not find people who are honest, trusting, empathetic, open, and faithful outside of the work environment who, by changing hats on the way to the office, become deceitful and untrustworthy. If you have the blinders off, your introspection should place you on the hierarchy of moral development at the same location, regardless of environment.

But what about those of you who have inadvertently found yourselves at an unethical place of business, or who work for superiors who place low on the hierarchy of moral development? What about those of you who say that no matter what the "higher-ups" are up to, you need to maintain job security and a certain standard of living—that you have no choice but to stay? Take it from us: There's no such thing as no choice. There's no reason to remain on a sinking ship, one that sooner or later will take you, your credibility, and your self-respect down with it. No job that requires you to behave unethically is worth it.

Howard Gardner, the John H. and Elisabeth A. Hobbs Professor of Cognition and Education at the Harvard Graduate School of Education, is seen as a foremost expert on ethical minds. Since 1995, he and teams of investigators at four universities have been researching the ways in which people aspire to do good work—that is, work of high quality that matters to society, enhances the lives of others, and is conducted in an ethical manner. "If you are not prepared to resign or be fired for what you believe in," Gardner states, "then you are not a worker, let alone a professional. You are a slave."

Find a company that has superior values and practices, no matter what.

Tracing the Moral Development of J. Barry Griswell

Barry would be the first to tell you that his formative experiences probably better prepared him for a life of crime than a life of personal and professional success. How he received the hard lessons that would later help lead him up the hierarchy of moral development and increase his business savvy is not the norm for successful people, and hardly a desirable way to gain a moral education. His learning is also testament to how experiential learning can actually occur many years later, once a person has advanced far enough in his thinking to correctly interpret early experiences.

One Sunday, when Barry was fourteen and not yet old enough to drive without an adult in the car, he persuaded his stepfather to let him drive the family car the few miles home from church alone. Along the way on a winding road he came upon a buddy in the car in front of him. Barry attempted to pass and the other driver recognized him and sped up. Just as he was whipping around a curve in the left lane, Barry met an oncoming car. There was no time to avoid a collision, and he hit the other car head-on. The car was occupied by his next-door neighbors—a father, mother, and several young children. Just minutes after the crash, Barry's parents and brother came upon the wreck. The family had survived, and Barry had escaped, injured but alive. His head lacerations required more than one hundred stitches. Over the next fifteen years glass that had been embedded in the side of his head would occasionally surface and need to be removed by a doctor, serving as a constant reminder of his incredibly irresponsible behavior.

Barry was just doing what was socially acceptable and even expected from the group he was running with—he was using stage 3 moral reasoning. But the tragic incident would eventually serve as an extremely powerful lesson. Later in his life, he began to conduct some honest introspection and was able to transform raw experience into experiential learning. Mainly, he learned that bad decisions almost always come with bad consequences. Earlier experiences, such as landing in a youth detention center, hadn't gotten through to him. But this one—whose bad consequence could've easily been death—did. The experience of the accident would come to serve as one of many catalysts for his move into stage 4 and eventually into postconventional moral reasoning. The consequences of his faulty moral reasoning were quite tangible: The victims of the accident lived right next door, and glass from the accident emerged for years. It was impossible to avoid the fact that major changes were in order. It's an example of how a painful situation can, with the use of accurate introspection, serve as a turning point for the journey up the hierarchy of moral development, which ultimately strengthens one's business savvy.

But advancing up the hierarchy of moral development doesn't happen overnight, and that was certainly the case in Barry's life. In fact, even as he went into college, he still found himself in stage 3 most of the time. Barry's main motivation was to be popular with friends and fit into the group. As a result he did what the crowd did, which included smoking, drinking, vandalism, getting into fights, and shoplifting. College was merely a means to play basketball, and his grades were mediocre at best. Over time, the negative consequences of his behavior began to accumulate. Barry's girlfriend at the time, Michele Irwin, broke up with him and even went so far as to transfer to a different school. Barry had looked up to her father, a Baptist minister, as a mentor, and now his mentor was sorely disappointed in him. Barry doubted that he could ever mend either relationship. Even basketball, until then one of his life's passions, started to lose its luster. All signs indicated that something was terribly amiss, and it was all too apparent that he was heading nowhere fast.

Barry struggled with the moral reasoning that was leading to his poor decisions and the negative consequences he was incurring. In essence, he realized he was stuck in stage 3 and that that level of moral reasoning was proving unsatisfactory. Faced with totally inadequate reasoning, he broadened his way of thinking and his subsequent behavior improved. He made the move up the hierarchy of moral development to stage 4.

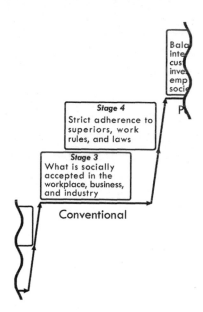

Other factors certainly played their part in leading Barry from stage 3 (social acceptance) to stage 4 (authority and rules prevail). There was the early moral education church provided—Barry's mother had made sure he was there every Sunday. There was his mother's insistence that he never, ever tell a lie. There was his college professor who awakened Barry to the world of business. Suddenly, school was no longer a means to play basketball, but basketball was a means to go to school. There was the desire to rebuild the relationship with his girlfriend, Michele.

The odds were stacked against Barry from the beginning. It would have been just as easy, if not easier, to become bitter about his tumultuous family life, to avoid responsibility for his actions, to take the path of least resistance and remain in a life of petty crime and low expectations. But mentors and other positive influences were there to help lead Barry up the hierarchy of moral development, and negative consequences were there as a visceral reminder that he was not pursuing the life he wanted and that he needed to make drastic changes. He learned to do the necessary introspection work that would enable him to turn even the worst experiences into experiential learning. And business, with its inevitable moral dilemmas, turned out to be the most influential instrument for leading himself up to the postconventional level.

For Barry the ending is a happy one. He not only graduated from college but also went on to earn his MBA. He pursued a career he enjoyed and at which he excelled. At the time of this writing, he is weeks away from retiring from a very successful career leading The Principal, which is 242nd on the Fortune 500 list, and transferring to a new job as the president of the Community Foundation of Greater Des Moines, an organization that works to improve the community's quality of life through philanthropy. Knowing firsthand the need for early positive influences, he is passionate about early childhood development and does all he can to support improving the odds for young people. He is a vocal proponent of ethical business practices, and his ethics have been acknowledged by his peers. In May 2007, *Ethisphere* magazine named The Principal Financial Group one of the world's most ethical companies.

And Michele Irwin? Luckily for Barry, she is now Michele Griswell.

The Gray Zone

Once you reach the postconventional stage of moral reasoning, making ethical decisions and resolving ethical dilemmas should be easy, right? How we wish that were the case! The truth is that the business world is full of moral dilemmas, and even with sound moral reasoning, matters will arise that fall into the so-called Gray Zone, a space rife with adversity. The Gray Zone encompasses not only those dilemmas that do not have a definitive right answer, but also those in which almost all decisions come at the detriment of someone or something else. Stockholders, those who provide the funds to operate and without whom you wouldn't have a business, could suffer. Or your employees, those who make your company go, could suffer. The list goes on and on and includes customers, your family, and parts or all of society. Faced with certain dilemmas, a manager cannot afford to stay at stage 4 (authority and laws prevail) for long, as stage 4 lacks the reasoning ability to deal with many of the thorny issues, problems, or opportunities routinely found in the business environment. The answers to these dilemmas do not come in books and it is difficult to teach how to balance so many interests.

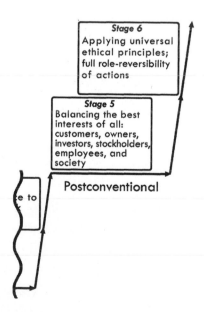

If there's any good news about the Gray Zone, which challenges even those at stages 5 and 6, it's that facing these especially problematic dilemmas facilitates advancement up the hierarchy of moral development and certainly the development of one's business savvy. And there's no end to the number of Gray Zone issues the businessperson will face, especially those in leadership positions. After all our years in business, we've found ourselves in the Gray Zone more times than we wish to recount. As our Look Backs and Postmortems indicate, we haven't always made the best decisions, but each experience has nudged us further up the hierarchy of moral development and has catalyzed improved moral reasoning, better decision making, and higher overall success. Gray Zone dilemmas are rarely published, as they're often troubling or embarrassing, but companies routinely face them, and we hope you'll learn from some of the Gray Zone dilemmas we've encountered.

In one case a leading sales representative got caught falsifying hotel receipts. Your recourse is simple, right? You just fire him. Problem is, he is a top producer, and firing him will hurt the bottom line and the stockholders. He is also well liked, so if he goes, you run the risk of losing some key customers. What's more, he's a friend, a company veteran who's been through thick and thin with you. If you fire him, what are you saying to other employees? That you had an unwritten "one strike and you're out" policy? That you don't value years of loyal and trusted service? But if you don't fire him, are you tacitly telling employees that it's okay to cheat? Now take it a step further: It turns out the employee was falsifying the receipts not for the money but to hide an affair he was having in another city. His behavior, while clearly unethical, hasn't cost the company a dime. So is business now to be concerned with and penalize a person for his conduct outside of work?

What would you do in the face of this kind of adversity? How do you find your way through the Gray Zone and arrive at the right decision?

In this case, the employee was fired, and the outcome was quite costly. Some sales that were in the representative's pipeline were lost, as were a couple of customers. And a valued friendship dissolved. But in the long run making the extremely difficult decision to fire the employee preserved the company's ethical standards, and it showed employees that management would abide by its principles. Eventually, sales returned. The long-term gain exceeded the short-term pain, and again we see the adversity paradox in action.

We've both dealt with multiple cases of managers who discriminated in one way or another, intentionally or unintentionally, for reasons of race, sex, religion, and even social class. Not taking quick action with reported discrimination cases can be costly on many levels. It can do inestimable damage to the individual who was discriminated against, it can harm your company culture and your employees' faith in management, and if the case makes it to court, the very least you can expect is that your company will emerge with a damaged reputation and some stiff penalties to pay. Management should be swift to address discrimination cases . . . but at the same time, make sure you hear both sides of the story. The accused person risks having his or her career and reputation destroyed, and he or she deserves a chance to voice a side of the story just as much as the accuser does. This is a very tricky and delicate situation for managers, one that clearly requires a deep reservoir of empathy and sharp moral reasoning skills.

In discrimination issues, it seems no two cases are alike. In one case a manager continually used racist and sexist language around a black female administrative assistant, and she made a complaint through the appropriate channels. The manager in question had been with the company more than fifteen years and was on his third promotion and move of his family. The allegation was too serious simply to scold, coach, or write up the manager or to transfer the manager or the administrative assistant. Clearly if the facts were true, he would need to be terminated. Upon investigation, it was found that the manager was mostly insensitive and needed training. The administrative assistant was given lots of support and empathy and offered the option of having her manager removed immediately or helping us work with him to get the needed training. She chose the latter. The manager was transferred out of a supervisory role so that no employees reported to him.

This case actually has a happy ending. The administrative assistant was pleased that her issue was swiftly addressed; the manager gained the training he clearly needed and performed well in his new job. Eventually the administrative assistant's husband transferred to another city and she left the company, but she remains in touch and sends Christmas cards every year.

The list of Gray Zone dilemmas we've personally faced goes on and on. Take, for instance, the manager struggling with production problems who committed suicide. How much responsibility should the company take, and how does one make the situation better without creating greater exposure for stockholders? Or how about catching agents or distributors making political contributions to obtain business? They are not on your payroll, so how much authority do you try to exercise over them when they are actually your customers? Then there was the case of the foreign subsidiary that paid bribes. Bribery was accepted practice in that country and arguably allowable under the U.S. Foreign Corrupt Practices Act, but is this the sort of person you want on your team? How about the sales representative who acknowledged stealing the trash of competitors to study competitive bids to gain the upper hand? Trash is public domain, stockholders were being rewarded, and some may even say the sales representative was being innovative, but what does that say about your corporate culture and what your company may be becoming?

Then you have sex, drugs, and alcohol issues in the workplace that enter the Gray Zone. How about the senior executive who was having an affair with his administrative assistant? Do your personal values come into play, and if so, to what degree? Then there was the tremendously valued, dedicated, and trustworthy employee who admitted to being an alcoholic. No problem, send him to a treatment program. The problem is, he refused. Now what? Do you terminate an employee whose personal problems aren't currently affecting his job performance, but who clearly needs help and whose problems are sure to show up at the office eventually?

Especially painful are the constant issues of reductions in work force (RIFs). Often dictated by market forces, not conducting RIFs when needed does not pay due respect to your stockholders. But doing RIFs undoubtedly creates havoc with the lives of fellow team members and their families.

There is a lot of anguish when working dilemmas in the Gray Zone, and there should be. The person who doesn't wrestle with Gray Zone dilemmas is not one you want on your team. Businesspeople with outstanding business savvy engage in proactive efforts to preclude these types of dilemmas before they arise, or at least nip them in the bud when they do.

And when ethical failures do happen, business-savvy professionals gain experiential learning and put the painful experience to work. Many companies promote diversity training to stamp out discrimination issues before they occur. Some become outstanding selectors and promoters of good people so as to build the savviest and most ethical teams from the very beginning. Still others spend an inordinate amount of time on strategic planning so reduction in workforce requirements are kept to a minimum. And most companies diligently develop processes geared toward avoiding company dilemmas that could enter the Gray Zone in the first place.

Suggestions to Help with Your Climb

The business you are in right now may be vital to your moving up the hierarchy of moral development. If your company has a moral compass and you are surrounded by morally developed individuals, there may be no better place to get your bearings and learn by example.

In our climbs we have been fortunate to receive a lot of helpful advice, especially when soul-searching while in the Gray Zone. CEOs of large companies are constantly entering the Gray Zone, and besides the advice of a management team, they often have three mirrors. There are, first, a trusted advisor within the organization, second, someone completely outside the organization, and third, a genuinely independent board. If people who have risen to the top of their organizations still need gut checks and a number of mirrors with which to triangulate, then it follows that employees at every level of business need the same assistance. CEO or copy clerk, the same diligence is required to climb the hierarchy of moral development. Set up a Value Team for yourself. Find a mentor within the business and a disinterested but knowledgeable party away from work. Set up your own board if you have to, composed of a group of trustworthy and discreet advisors.

The value of having multiple mentors of one type or another cannot be underestimated, but there are also "mental mentors" you can use to help guide your decisions and behavior. Ask yourself if your mother or father would approve or disapprove of your behavior or decision. Or behave as if your actions and decisions will be detailed on the front page of the morning paper. We've all heard stories about politicians, celebrities, or business speakers wearing remote microphones and saying the wrong things when they didn't realize the mic was still on. You can conduct your life as if you are wearing a microphone and you just never know when it might really be on. These mental mentors are not in place to help you avoid embarrassment (though that's a happy side effect). The point in employing them is to develop values and behavior that your mother or father would approve of, that you'd be proud for the paper to publish, and that what would be broadcast over the loudspeaker would be a credit to your reputation. In all cases, your behavior should match your values. Eventually, you'll make your way up the hierarchy of moral development, and superior moral reasoning will become such a habit that you'll no longer have a need for these mental mentors.

The Adversity Paradox Takeaways:
Where Are You on the Hierarchy of Moral Development?

- Stated values may not mean a whole lot—look at Enron. It's behavior that gives a true indication of who you really are. In the best-case scenario, your stated values are always in accordance with your actual behavior. Ethical behavior is a function of adequate moral reasoning, which is indicated by how far you have climbed on the hierarchy of moral development.
- Using the skill of introspection, ascertain your position on the hierarchy of moral development. As you do so, keep these guiding principles in mind:
  — Over 50 percent of people are at the conventional level (stages 3 and 4).
  — One cannot skip stages in development.
  — Regression is unusual.
  — The moral person and the moral businessperson are one and the same.
- If you are not at the level you need to be, determine your goal and ways to climb.
- Evaluate the flock with whom you fly. Do you need to adjust the flock to assist your climb? Do you have the resolve to do so?
- Do you have the triangulation needed to climb the hierarchy of moral development?

6

Work Character—Sorry, but There's No Substitute for Hard Work:
Human Capital Component No. 3

One morning we took a random, very informal, and unscientific survey of the people we happened to encounter. "What comes to mind when you think of the term 'work ethic?'" we asked. We heard some answers again and again: hard work or hard labor, long hours, diligence, dedication. Other responses included putting your nose to the grindstone, perseverance, concentrated effort, commitment to work, and working with discipline.

We then asked the same people a follow-up question: "What comes to mind when you think of work *character?*" With that question, we got a quizzical look and pretty much the same answer from everyone: "It's the same thing . . . right?"

"Work ethic" and "work character" are certainly related—both have to do with applying yourself wholeheartedly to a job or task—but work character is a broader category. The word "character" originates in the Greek word *kharakter,* which means "stamping tool." A stamping tool makes a *distinctive mark,* which is the earliest English meaning of "character." Eventually, the word took on the nuance of token feature or trait or distinguishing quality. People with a fully developed work character are qualitatively different from their peers: Their excellent work habits and the success they earn distinguish them from the pack. The idea of *work character* in *The Adversity Paradox* is rooted in this distinguishing quality that encompasses a person's attitude *and* ability. People with an outstanding work character habitually work hard, think hard, and lead well—and because they're pursuing what they love, they enjoy their work. We'll be looking at "work character" through three specific lenses: your *physical work ethic,* your *cognitive work ethic,* and your *skills to lead.*

Physical Work Ethic

One's *physical work ethic* is simply the ability and the willingness to engage in physical labor to gain a specified outcome. Here is where we draw closest to the most common understanding of "work ethic." What comes to mind when you picture a person with a superior physical work ethic? An athlete training ten hours a day? A medical intern slogging through thirty-six-hour shifts on no sleep? A construction worker jackhammering concrete in the hot sun until the job is done? A farmhand working dawn to dusk? They're all correct answers. Every one of these people is engaged in demanding physical labor, which is what tends to come to mind when one thinks of a physical work ethic. But having a well-developed physical work ethic isn't limited to those who break a sweat. Anything, and we repeat anything, that requires discipline, dedication, diligence, and perseverance to be successful requires a strong physical work ethic. The scholar who spends hour upon hour in research and study also has a robust physical work ethic. Likewise, the businessperson who consistently gives her best efforts and then some, who puts in more hours and effort than is expected, has a superior physical work ethic. Simply stated, people with a well-developed physical work ethic have the ability and the willingness to put in the requisite hours and effort to do a job to their fullest potential.

Lots of books will give you advice on marketing, leadership, selling, business planning, and so on. And certainly anyone trying to succeed in business needs sound business advice and practices, but an often overlooked aspect of succeeding involves the physical demands of business. Developing a physical work ethic is critical to the business savvy: You need energy and stamina to provide the effort it takes to be successful. If you don't have the sheer physical ability to put in the time and effort, you're at a disadvantage from the start. Think of the entrepreneur or the executive in a leadership position—there's really no such thing as quitting time. Think of the sales representative who relentlessly pounds the pavement with no predetermined start or stop times. How about those who leave the office with their briefcase full every night and on the weekends? Those routinely sending work e-mails at 10:00 P.M. or 6:00 A.M.? The fact is, any of you who are trying to move up the corporate ladder will be required to put in whatever extra hours and effort are necessary in order to distinguish yourself from the pack. If you're not physically up to the task, or if you're operating at half speed, you're going to be at a significant disadvantage from the beginning.

Those in leadership roles may have even more of a responsibility to develop a strong physical work ethic. We've never known a good leader who didn't work extraordinarily hard and set a good work ethic example for his or her team members. Good leaders know that their team members will emulate them; it's their job to set the standard for productivity. If the team sees the leader slacking off, they'll follow suit and start performing at a level at or below the leader's. Further, anyone who fails to work hard is in danger of being passed by for hiring or promotions, or outright termination. This is the stark reality of the business world. In fact, we've never known a person who avoided the development of his or her physical work ethic and achieved real success.

Cognitive Work Ethic

A cognitive work ethic is engagement of the mind to learn, solve problems, find opportunities, develop solutions, or successfully execute the tasks a job requires. Here again, a cognitive work ethic is ecumenical—it applies to all jobs. You wouldn't necessarily think of a mechanic in a manufacturing plant as needing a superior cognitive work ethic to be good at what he does, but is he not engaging his mind to execute successfully all kinds of tasks? He must know intricate details of complicated machinery, how to use it, how to maintain it, and what to do when it breaks down. Though the mechanic may often need to rely heavily on his physical work ethic and the financial analyst may rely more heavily on his cognitive work ethic, every successful worker needs well-developed physical and cognitive work ethics. Mental work can be just as strenuous and fatiguing as physical work.

The need for a fully developed cognitive work ethic for any type of success is growing more pronounced every day. At one time there were plenty of jobs in factories or on the farm in which physical work ethic requirements prevailed, and many paid quite well. Today, one robot replaces five or more jobs and one worker can service a dozen robots. Likewise, one worker with a good physical and cognitive work ethic has replaced a substantial number of workers who once relied solely on their physical work ethic for fulfilling needs. Over time, unemployment in America has remained relatively unchanged, but much of the workforce has been required to move from employing their physical work ethic to using their cognitive work ethic to earn a living.

In today's business world, a robust cognitive work ethic is required simply to stay in the game, much less excel. Business is more complex and conducted at a faster pace than ever before. This requires one to think harder, faster, with more focus, and for more hours of the day. One must stay apprised of constantly changing technologies, the vicissitudes of the market, the overall health of one's own business (not to mention the competition's), and maintain familiarity with a business world that reaches to the far corners of the globe. Even entry-level business positions now require a college degree—and with good reason.

Skills to Lead

A physical work ethic is the ability and the willingness to conduct sustained physical effort. You're not going to get ahead without the ability to conduct physically demanding work. Working smart for greater results requires the development of sustained mental effort, the cognitive work ethic. These two elements of work character are essential for success. But even with the most highly developed physical and cognitive work ethics, one person can do only so much on his or her own.

Our friend Ron Willingham told a great story that perfectly illustrates the concept. The cleaner 20-Mule Team Borax has been around for more than a hundred years. The box features a twenty-mule team pulling two huge wagons and a smaller one out of a borax pit in Death Valley, California. It was years before Ron discovered the significance of the picture. For many years wagoners used twelve mules to pull the wagonload of borax from an open pit to a railroad several miles away, and no one questioned it. Then a creative thinker who wasn't content to live with conventional wisdom began experimenting. He found that by adding eight mules to the twelve he more than doubled their pulling capacity. It created new power.

That's synergy. Where two or more people or forces work together in a cooperative spirit, the total power becomes greater than the sum of the individual powers. That's how teams work. When synchronized, teams of people can do exponentially more than the combined efforts of individuals, each acting alone. Obviously, with teams comes the need for leadership. Leadership skills are geared toward moving the masses and multiplying efforts. They are essential for screening, molding, fitting, and stitching groups of people into teams of skills and talent and then directing them efficiently. Leadership and the teamwork that results from it are easily the largest differentiators between like companies.

"Skills to lead," the third part of work character, brings us into more specialized territory. It can uniquely combine any number of skills. Certainly it can involve things like effective public speaking, communication, team selection, team building, an ability to motivate others, delegation, and having good vision, but "skills to lead" is an adaptable concept. That is, one's skills to lead will depend on the people one is leading, the business one is in, and the corporate culture. It requires a different set of skills to lead a corporation of 20,000 employees than it does to lead a small business of seven, or to lead the business that must be quick and nimble versus the environment that rewards the steady-Eddie, low-cost producer. Effective leaders have maximized the development of their physical and cognitive work ethics, and they know how to lead their particular business. Another important philosophy is the idea that true leadership is about stewardship. Dr. Robert L. Joss, Philip K. Knight Professor and dean of the Graduate Business School at Stanford University, was interviewed by *Fast Company* back in 2003. Dean Joss had an excellent response to the question "What matters most and why?" "I have one word for you," he said. "Leadership. By leadership, I mean taking complete responsibility for an organization's well-being and growth and changing it for the better. Real leadership is not about prestige, power, or status. It's about responsibility." We also find this excerpt from Dean Joss's welcoming address to GBS students both encouraging and quite meaningful: "Leadership is a noble calling. . . . In addition to meeting well-defined strategic objectives, leaders must also help their organizations make meaningful contributions to social issues, economic growth, and political stability. That's why effective organizational leadership plays a vital role in shaping our world." A truly great leader's efforts will be felt in his or her business and beyond.

The full work character package consists of a combination of physical work ethic, cognitive work ethic, and the additional skills of leadership that multiply your efforts. Later in this chapter we'll meet two businesspeople who used their physical and cognitive work ethics to start businesses from scratch, and then added skills to help grow those businesses into enormous successes.

Working Not Just Harder but Better: Enhancing Your Physical and Cognitive Work Ethics

Anyone can tell you to work harder or to think harder in order to improve your business or your career trajectory—you've probably said as much to yourself. But how do you actually *do* it? Realizing that one needs to work harder or perform better doesn't automatically translate into increased output on a continuing basis, nor does it even mean that some people *begin* the process of improvement. We can have the best of intentions, but if we have no idea how to start or follow through on them, we're stuck at square one. So we'd like to provide you with three proven processes that have worked in our own lives to promote positive change:

1. Motivation/visualization
2. Adding "And Then Some" to everything you do
3. Successful habits

Motivation/Visualization

If you ask most people what gets them out of bed and to the office every morning, they'll have a quick answer: the paycheck. Every single one of us needs to make a living, but it's a sad state of affairs when the *only* reason we go to work is for the money. However, let's imagine, just for a moment, that you're in one of those jobs that's pure drudgery, that money is the only reason you remain at your job. In this bleak situation, what could possibly motivate you to work harder and perform better?

Let us take one answer off the table right now—more money. More dollars might bring you a bit more spending power, a few new things, but those are temporary highs. More money isn't likely to be a permanent motivating factor. And according to recent surveys, money is actually pretty far down the list of what motivates people to perform well at a job or remain at a place of employment.

What *does* consistently motivate employees lies in the area of the intangible. A recent Gallup study found that recognition of one's efforts has the largest impact on worker engagement and performance. Other huge motivating factors include a sense of self-worth, a feeling of accomplishment, the satisfaction of taking part in meaningful work, the sense of being a part of a vibrant and accomplished team, or pursuing a more challenging role with greater responsibility. Or let's revisit that awful job for just a moment: Maybe your biggest motivating factor is getting out of that job and into one that provides the kind of long-lasting intangible rewards we've listed here. These are the kinds of motivating factors that we're talking about. What you need is something powerful enough, something *meaningful* enough, that it gets you working and thinking at such a level that you won't rest until you attain your goal.

Now, we're fully aware that for some, money is the sole motivating factor, and for good reason. Barry found himself in this position early on; his family needed money for basic necessities, and he did what he had to do to make it. Goals such as self-fulfillment and recognition for his efforts were far down his list of priorities, if they were present at all. He was simply providing a service in exchange for a paycheck; his motivating factor was money, or more correctly, survival.

Abraham Maslow's well-known hierarchy of needs theory illustrates the concept perfectly. As individuals meet basic needs, they seek to satisfy higher needs that occupy a set hierarchy, which Maslow illustrated with a pyramid diagram:

Maslow's Hierarchy of Needs

As lower needs on the pyramid are met, one is free to move up to higher, more abstract needs. Once a basic level of security was established and Barry was free from the anxiety of living a subsistence-level existence, he was able to concentrate on fulfilling needs higher on the pyramid, such as achievement, confidence, and self-esteem. Wherever you find yourself on your career path, there's your starting point. Identify your number-one motivating factor, the driving force that will guarantee you will increase your performance and productivity, and don't rest until you reach your goal. If you can keep your focus and continually enhance your work character, you'll soon be working not just for a paycheck (the bottom level of the pyramid), but for more of the intangible goals that will be meaningful for a lifetime.

Of course, the most powerful motivating factor of all arrives when you've found a purpose you can pursue with passion and bring to fruition through your career. We'll be looking at purpose and passion in detail in the next chapter, but here suffice it to say that when one has found a way to put one's purpose to work, work ceases to be work and all the motivation you'll ever need comes effortlessly from within. People who work in service professions often report the highest job satisfaction, and this has everything to do with the fact that they've found a way to put their purpose to work and that they're helping others. (By the way, the professions with the highest job satisfaction? The clergy, firefighters, and physical therapists, in that order. The lowest? Manual laborers, food preparers, and hand packers and packagers, with manual laborers being the least satisfied.) It doesn't matter what career you're in as long as you're living out your purpose. As long as you've put your purpose to work, any profession can come with its own built-in motivation and a high degree of self-fulfillment and satisfaction.

Now as for visualization, think of it as a helping hand to motivation. Many people have found visualizing their goal—keeping an image of it constantly before them—extremely helpful. Before we proceed, a word of caution: There are plenty of people out there who confer too much power on visualization, as if merely seeing a satisfied goal in your mind's eye produces that result. We're not of that school. Visualization is a means, not an end.

But it can be a very powerful means. How does one use it? If your motivating goal is to own and run your own company, picture yourself in that role. Let your mental image be as specific as possible—the more detailed your vision, the more real it will be and the more you'll want it, and the more motivated you'll be in attaining it. So literally visualize yourself in the office or conference room of your dreams, surrounded by an enthusiastic, dedicated, highly skilled and happy team. Visualize the bottom line you want to achieve, the service awards you and your team will garner, the fabulous customer feedback you'll receive. Visualize it until it's as real as this book in your hands, maintain that vision, and then consider it inevitable that you'll make that vision a reality.

Visualization can help with any goal. If you want to manage your company's regional office, picture yourself not only promoted to the position, but also as the best-producing regional manager the company has ever had. If you want to be the top sales representative in your company, visualize yourself standing on the podium receiving the plaque, your superior effort being recognized by a standing ovation. Bob used visualization to become a more confident, effective public speaker. How? He simply visualized the outcome he desired; namely, he saw himself in front of a large group of people, speaking with confidence and clarity. He visualized a raptly attentive audience and plenty of applause at the end of his speech. He visualized with enough frequency and fervency that his desired outcome came to seem inevitable. By the time he actually took the stage, he had rehearsed the scenario so much all he had to do was step into the role.

Noted businessman and bestselling author Harvey Mackay understood his work character development as well as anyone we talked to, and he instinctively used visualization from the time he was a child. Mackay had a typical laundry list of jobs in his youth that we saw with so many we profiled. He had a paper route, sold magazines door to door, shoveled snow, mowed lawns, clerked in a men's store, and caddied on weekends at the local golf course. "Of all the jobs I've ever had," Mackay said, "my paper route taught me the most. Getting up seven days a week at four A.M. to deliver papers by six taught me hard work. I learned the art of thinking about how I would reward myself with my earnings, which kept me focused on the job in front of me." Mackay recalls how he could always visualize and feel the awards in his mind well before he achieved them. Even as a child he says he dreamed of one day owning his own factory. "It didn't matter what it would manufacture," he said. "I just visualized myself walking up and down the aisles and having people, my team, making products and smiling at me."

Already ahead of the game with his physical and cognitive work ethics, and with more than enough visualization-fueled motivation to succeed, Mackay felt confident enough at the age of twenty-six to purchase an insolvent envelope manufacturer with twelve employees and outdated equipment. Manufacturing and selling a commodity for a profit is always a tough business. It is very difficult to differentiate products, and the barriers for others to enter the business are very low. But Mackay grew his business from its meager beginnings to more than $100 million in sales and 600 employees. Mackay writes and speaks extensively on the lessons he learned as he grew the company—everything he learned about salesmanship, management, motivation, and negotiation—and has authored several very successful books. The boy on a bike who visualized his success found it, and then some.

Adding "And Then Some" to Everything You Do

Sometimes it's worthwhile to state the obvious, and such is the case here. Apply the power of "and then some" to everything you do, and you're guaranteed to get positive results. Set your goals higher than what is expected of you and find ways to achieve them.

It helps to identify specific goals or specific areas you want to work on. If you're supposed to make ten cold calls, make fifteen. If your quota is to make x amount of commission, add 10 percent to that and make it. Next quarter, add another 10 percent. Sometimes, setting a goal arises directly out of identifying a weakness or lack—or having one identified for you. Maybe a performance review points out that you're not a team player. Or maybe your quarterly sales report reveals that you've fallen far short of your projected sales goals. Maybe you lack some sort of technical knowledge that would make your performance more effective or make you more competitive for a promotion. Or maybe you've got your eye on a new job, and a little research indicates that you're weak in a certain area the company wants. Or maybe you're a member of a large team and you're getting lost in the pack and you want to distinguish yourself.

We could provide a chapter's worth of examples. The beauty of the power of "and then some" is that it can apply to any situation. You can apply the power of "and then some" to literally anything you want to accomplish, and positive results are sure to follow. This one's a no-brainer. If you're completing your tasks *and then some,* if you're putting in the extra effort required to distinguish yourself from your peers, there's no way you can't advance. The trick is to make "and then some" a lifelong habit.

Just think of where you could end up if you *habitually* go above and beyond, instead of doing just *enough to get by.* Think of where your employees and therefore your company could go if you modeled the power of "and then some" every day on the job. Think of where your kids could go if you are teaching them to rely on the power of "and then some," never to settle for doing just *enough to get by.*

Unfortunately, so many experiences in life go the way of just *enough to get by.* How often do we begin a new endeavor on fire with enthusiasm and vigor, with every intention of wowing everyone with our performance and changing our lives for the better? At the outset of a project—whether it be a class, a hobby, a job assignment, or even a diet—we're more than happy to throw in all our effort *and then some.* But so often, we end up settling for only taking these newfound opportunities to a slightly higher level at best. We do just *enough to get by,* and perhaps most unfortunate, we demonstrate a minimum level of acceptable performance to our kids. Who knows what our sons and daughters could achieve if we weren't to set the bar too low or teach them the art of *enough to get by?*

The difference between employing *enough to get by* and *and then some* may hardly be visible within a given task or in a day's work, but over a lifetime it can be the largest separator between a life of mediocrity and a life of success.

Successful Habits

The third way you can make positive change is by making hard work not just a short-term means to reach a short-term goal, but a lifetime modus operandi. This is about how, using the power of "and then some," you can create and incorporate habits that ensure a lifetime of success.

Early in his career selling insurance, Barry's company provided him with an essay called "The Common Denominator of Success," written by Albert E. N. Gray, which proved to be enormously influential. "I still keep a copy of it today," Barry said, "and I still swear by its wisdom." Gray was with the Prudential Insurance Company of America back in the 1940s when he wrote the essay, which posited that the common denominator of success was that the successful formed a habit of doing things that failures don't like to do. Barry took Gray's words to heart.

"There were a lot of others working very hard at insurance sales when I was trying to get started, and most of us did the same things," Barry said. "The difference was my picking up on those things they did not like to do and habitually making them a part of my routine." As a sales manager, Barry discovered that the single most important and difficult activity was recruiting top-notch salespeople. He attacked the task with "and then some" and threw himself into recruiting. He worked every Saturday morning, and he used every Sunday night to prepare for the coming week. He also employed a system that he still uses to this day to ensure that he would get everything, even the most unpleasant of tasks, completed. "I make a running list of things I need to get done within the next two weeks to thirty days," he said. "Then I code every item as A, must do, B, need to do, and C, would like to do. The key is to start with the As and get them all done, move on to the Bs—and rarely get to the Cs. The unsuccessful tend to knock off the Cs and maybe a few Bs but rarely get to the As, and never all of them."

There was one more item from Gray's essay that stuck with Barry for life. Gray asked, "Why are some able to do things they don't like to do while others are not? Because they have a purpose strong enough to make them form the habit of doing things they don't like to do in order to accomplish the purpose they want to accomplish." Have you noticed how this topic of purpose keeps coming up? It's no accident!

Whereas forming habits that make you successful may seem like drudgery, once they become habits they are no longer a grind, especially when you start enjoying the rewards of the success you have created with them. The same is true for all this talk of working and thinking hard. Once you've found a purpose you can be passionate about, work is no longer work. This doesn't mean that you still won't work hard, but working hard will not be a burden, because you'll love what you do.

Let's now shift our discussion back to the third component of work character, skills to lead. We'd like to introduce you to two savvy businesspeople whose skills to lead, when added to their already strong physical and cognitive work ethics, made for businesses that have become models of success.

Doris Christopher

When Doris Christopher started the Pampered Chef, she already had both her physical and cognitive work ethics in place. Her business would not have gotten off the ground without them. Adept at introspection even before starting her business, she took inventory of her skills and interests to help analyze what she wanted and could do for a part-time career. She had cooking expertise she'd learned at home, in school, and then with years of observation and experimentation. She was educated to teach and had teaching experience. She had a keen understanding of hospitality and entertaining. She also had the family values including love, respect, and trust instilled in her by her parents and practiced within her own family.

What she didn't have was business skills or experience, and she'd never managed employees. This is where a highly developed physical and cognitive work ethic came in very handy. Christopher had the stamina and the mental acuity to give herself a veritable crash course in business. "You must be realistic about what you're good at, what you can be good at, and then go get help where needed," Christopher said. "When I went into business, I had little or no business skills. This included accounting, marketing, sales, human resources, legal, and how to motivate people." She also lacked financial resources. But again Christopher's physical and cognitive work ethics came into play. She found money, although a meager amount, through her husband's insurance policy, and used it to finance inventory. She found her way into the Merchandise Mart in Chicago to source her products and learned how to manage an inventory closely with her limited financial resources. Her new skills in finance, purchasing, and inventory management may have been weak at first, but they steadily improved with usage.

Christopher's first kitchen show had sales of $178. It's a bottom line that would inspire most people to self-pity or discouragement, but Christopher, in fact, was joyful and optimistic. She viewed that first $178 as nothing less than success. But $178 is a far cry from the $700 million plus in sales the Pampered Chef makes annually. How did Christopher move from such a humble start to such an outstanding outcome? One part of the process was adding *skills to lead* to her total work character package.

Christopher's Skill to Lead No. 1: Culture Creator

The Pampered Chef's overwhelming success has drawn many business imitators. If Christopher could do it on $3,000, most believe the barriers to entry are very low. Christopher herself has learned to accept those who try to copy the Pampered Chef's business model, treating their imitations as a compliment. What imitators miss is the corporate culture that Christopher has built, something that cannot be bought or faked. Creating a viable corporate culture for a particular business is a specialized skill to lead. In Christopher's case, she modeled the business around what she knew—family and good old-fashioned family values.

"Early on," she said, "when the Pampered Chef was a one-woman show, my personal standards of ethical conduct were the standards that the business followed. The values I respected—integrity, determination, hard work, and respect for others—set the tone. Later, I had to communicate those values so everyone would know what was expected of him or her. I had to weave those values into the very fabric of the company." As her business grew, outside business advisors would have had her change her management structure, style, and methods, but Christopher stayed with her forte. Embracing change while maintaining values, she and her coworkers developed business processes that maintained the family culture and adopted a mission statement that reflected those values:

> We are committed to providing opportunities for individuals to develop their God-given talents and skills to their fullest potential to the benefit of themselves, their families, our customers, and the company. We are dedicated to enhancing the quality of family life by providing quality kitchen products, supported by service and information for our Consultants and customers.

The use of the first-person plural is no accident. Christopher consistently uses the word "we" when speaking about the Pampered Chef, and she means the entire Pampered Chef family. She describes how important such things as mutual respect and recognizing that everyone's job is important are in the Pampered Chef culture. "One thing about a company that should never be subject to change is its principles," she said. "While we are quick to embrace change, we never compromise our values and principles."

And change did occur. When the business was small, Christopher was able to know all the coworkers and Kitchen Consultants intimately. She knew the names of their spouses and children. She wrote personal notes on commission checks and called everyone on their birthdays and anniversaries and during the holiday season. Creating the culture with the start-up business was not difficult—it was simply Doris Christopher being who she is and bringing her own values and personal touches to the business. Being committed to that corporate culture and being able to expand it to a thousand employees were the greater challenges. It's at exactly this juncture that many businesses fail.

They are unable to perpetuate or even recognize the culture with which they found success.

The Pampered Chef succeeded here because of Christopher's leadership. Though the personal notes and calls are no longer possible given the size of the company, Christopher maintains the culture with which she started by adapting it to a much larger scale. "It starts by leading by example," she said. She gives a warm greeting to everyone she sees, saying hello to everyone she passes in the halls. "In doing so as the company leader," she said, "I believe I am setting the example for everyone else." The celebratory phone calls for birthdays and anniversaries have been replaced by one big coworker celebration every month. "These celebrations help create a sense of togetherness," she said, "a feeling of family in the workplace." A key leadership skill Christopher has been able to develop is the ability to develop and perpetuate a unique culture.

Christopher's Skill to Lead No. 2: People Selection

As discussed in chapter one, the business savvy are always aware of what they do not know, and they know the best way to deal with those voids in their knowledge. Christopher reeled off a number of potential skills she could have developed, such as accounting, marketing, and human resources, and there is no question that as the Pampered Chef grew so did her knowledge. But becoming a maven in areas like accounting and marketing was not the best way to multiply her efforts; as leader, her job was to find the people with those skills and to build synergistic teams.

Yet another reason to develop her skill in people selection was to prevent employee losses. Especially in a corporate culture of family and team, coworker failures were painful. Parting ways with those who did not work out was mentally akin to getting a divorce. After a few painful separations, Christopher and her management team quickly became adept at people selection. The Pampered Chef relies on three important selection elements. The first is determining whether a person has the qualifications to do the job. In cases where she believes she is not technically astute enough to make the judgment, she lets those who are qualify candidates. The second is trust: Can the person fit well into an intimate family environment? The third thing Christopher and her team consider is whether a candidate can "buy into the Pampered Chef's mission and vision." Technical qualifications alone aren't sufficient at the Pampered Chef. A candidate must be fully capable of fitting in, of being a team player and family member. Christopher learned a variety of tactics, such as verifying her analysis with other coworkers who interviewed candidates. Probing details on résumés and taking candidates to dinner to get an understanding of who they are outside the business environment is another technique Christopher uses. What better way to determine whether a candidate can fit into the Pampered Chef family than by having them sit down to a meal?

Christopher's Skill to Lead No. 3: Motivation of Others

In Christopher's very first kitchen show she realized how the positive reinforcement she received was so invigorating. In her ascent to the top there were some disappointments along the way, but she was amazed how quickly they faded when she received praise. She took the lesson to heart. "We constantly praise and recognize our people for their performances," she said. "I like to say we praise people to success."

Each year the Pampered Chef brings Kitchen Consultants to Chicago, where Christopher addresses thousands at a time. Having started the business working on the front lines, she has the empathy for her Kitchen Consultants that few, if any, CEOs have with frontline company representatives. Fear of public speaking was something that troubled Christopher in her early days. Though she may still get a little nervous, she no longer sees her task as burdensome; she sees it as an opportunity to speak with people she knows well and who are her family.

Like many companies, the Pampered Chef has incentive programs. Kitchen Consultants with high sales are awarded trips for two, coupled with awards banquets and other activities. Thresholds for winning are set so that anyone has the opportunity to achieve them. It is not always about spending a lot of money. It is about the little things—the public recognition, the awards, thanking the spouses and friends of achievers, and then adding all the personal touches. When employees know you care, Christopher believes, they care even more. At sales award banquets some attendees resemble decorated war veterans, a real honor in this corporate culture.

Doris Christopher began the Pampered Chef with a strong physical and cognitive work ethic—both of which grew stronger as her business became more demanding and she gained more experience. But it was her development of the third component of work character, her skills to lead, that enabled her to exponentially grow and manage a large business. Her unique leadership skill set consists of developing and perpetuating a unique culture, people selection; and motivation of others.

William J. Doré

Bill Doré may not be a familiar name to you unless you are involved with marine construction or are a fellow Horatio Alger member. At the time of this writing Doré is in the process of retiring from his position as CEO of Global Industries, Ltd., which is a leading provider of marine construction and support services.

To understand Doré's success with Global Industries you need to go back to his college days. He was an education major at McNeese State University, intent on becoming a teacher and a coach. By the end of his sophomore year he was married and had two kids. To pay the bills he drove an eighteen-wheeler in the evenings, making deliveries for a hardware store. During his junior year he switched to selling insurance, and by the time he graduated from college he was making far more with his part-time insurance sales than he could someday as a teacher and a coach. After acquiring a master's degree in education, he earned his real estate and securities licenses to expand on his insurance sales. Then in 1970, at the age of twenty-seven, he made a sales proposal for a mutual fund to a business owner. The owner declined, but was so impressed with Doré's salesmanship he offered him a job. It was a small diving company and the owner wanted to start a rental company to lease their idle diving equipment. By this time Doré had four kids, and his wife was sick with hepatitis. Gaining security for his family was paramount, and petroleum-related construction in the Gulf of Mexico was growing, so he took the job.

In 1972, Doré bought a 49 percent stake in the business with $8,000 he borrowed from his in-laws. By 1973, the equipment rental business was flourishing while an oil glut had caused the diving business to go into the tank. The majority owner offered Doré a proposition whereby Doré would take full ownership of the near-insolvent, three-employee diving company in exchange for his original investment. Diving revenue had dwindled to $200,000 while the rental company had blossomed to $1,500,000. It appeared to be a crazy move, but the lure of running his own business and the fear of later regretting his not seizing the opportunity were too great for Doré. Over time, Doré's crazy move paid off: He transformed the struggling diving company into a full-service offshore construction firm of 3,000 employees operating one of the largest fleets of marine construction assets in the world. Today Global Industries construction services extend throughout the Gulf of Mexico, West Africa, the Mediterranean, Middle East and India, Asia Pacific, South America, and Mexico's Bay of Campeche.

Doré's physical work ethic developed when he was young. His dad believed in his earning his own way, and money was tight. He had a full complement of jobs as an adolescent—shining shoes, cutting lawns, delivering newspapers, and spraying automobiles for mosquitoes at the local drive-in theater. Doré carried his physical work ethic into sports. As a senior in high school, he earned multiple scholarships for track and football.

The roots of Doré's cognitive work ethic can be found in his youth. "I had cousins on both sides of the family," he said. "Those on my mother's side went to school and everyone received a high school education. On my father's side no one went to school. They were all illiterate or nearly so. I could see the differences in their standards of living and knew I wanted more out of life." Doré is still an avid proponent of education. In 2001 he created, and is the sole supporter of, a Louisiana scholarship program through the Horatio Alger Association. Doré personally contributes fifty $10,000 scholarships annually. That's $500,000 to education, every single year.

Doré's Skill to Lead No.1: Team Coaching

In the early years of Global Industries, management was relatively uncomplicated. A small "family" worked closely together, doing whatever was necessary to secure a shared goal—survival, as Doré puts it. Long hours, shared failures, adversities to overcome, as well as successes achieved molded the Global Industries team into a close-knit group, creating a clear sense of mutual responsibility and trust. As the company grew from a handful of employees to a few hundred, Doré recognized that he needed to seek new ways to maintain the teamwork ethos so vital to his company's success.

He looked for concepts that helped him succeed in his own life. He'd learned the value of teamwork on the football field, and he borrowed lessons from this experience and applied them to the new challenges he faced managing Global Industries. In the process he realized his boyhood dream of becoming a coach by organizing his business much like a football team.

"I was never in a large corporation," said Doré, "so I could not identify with the corporate world's definition of team. I developed slides showing an offensive line, a defensive line, and backs, aligning these positions with accounting, human resources, management, estimating, contracts, and operations. They all have a purpose and must all work together in order to succeed." The company newsletter is appropriately named *The Coach* and its approach is to share the game plan.

The coaching and football team–style of management goes well beyond the coach. Workers are valued players and are encouraged to learn multiple positions. Like team dinners, there are employee dinners. And if conflicts arise between divisions at Global Industries, the players are called to "practice": Divers and barge operators are placed together on teams and given problems to solve together, the same as football team scrimmages.

The "winning team" analogy provided a common language for employees in describing their values and responsibilities as members of the Global Industries team. What kept such analogies from sounding strained or even trite was the example set by the head coach in his treatment of his players. Doré has the same love and respect for his players that good coaches do. They also share in the excitement, the pride, and the profits from the team's extended winning streak in the offshore construction market. "When our employees reach retirement age, I would like for them to feel they made the right choice in joining Global Industries and staying with us during the good and the bad times," Doré said. "Hopefully, they'll feel they invested their working lives on the right team and with the right coach."

Doré's Skill to Lead No. 2: Innovation

One might ask how innovation can turn from being a skill or talent to being a leadership skill. For companies that, by their very nature, must be innovative to survive, leadership has to lead by example. Offshore construction, sometimes more than two hundred miles from shore and more than a thousand feet below the surface, thrives on innovation.

Global Industries and innovation were synonymous the day Doré took over. The company and Doré had no money to speak of, so Doré borrowed an old thirty-foot trailer from a customer to use as an office. Another business colleague let him use a lot in Harvey, Louisiana, rent-free to house the borrowed trailer and the diving equipment. He obtained a $2,000 loan for working capital with the loan guarantee made by his in-laws. Customers required Global Industries to have insurance in order to do contract work, which had a hefty price tag of $40,000. Doré persuaded the insurance company to finance the premium. He had no way to load and unload equipment in the yard. He rented, for one dollar a year, a broken-down winch truck from a neighbor. It had a frozen engine and no windshield. He enlisted his father's help to get it running.

All this innovation and Global Industries was still not considered a going business concern. New codes for diving equipment had been adopted by the Coast Guard. Deep diving required saturation diving, which allowed divers to work in deep water for long periods of time. Saturation diving required expensive decompression chambers that enabled divers to decompress slowly from the pressures encountered on the ocean bottom as they returned to the surface. Global's first decompression chambers did not meet code, and a major capital investment was required to upgrade. Three months after the purchase Doré used some innovative sales methods, his forte, to land a $300,000 contract to provide diving inspection services. With the contract in hand, he was able to secure a $250,000 loan from the Small Business Administration to replace out-of-code equipment.

As Doré grew the business, the culture of innovation continued. The original Global Industries provided only diving services, which was just a piece of offshore construction work. The offshore industry in the Gulf was already twenty-five years old and there were several large companies dominating the supply of full construction services. These companies had financial resources and sophisticated equipment while Global Industries was barely on the map and had a single niche service. The market for construction services was also changing. Up to this point the petroleum industry had found and produced oil from under three hundred feet of water. The industry was headed for deeper water.

Doré wanted to go there, too, and not only that, he wanted to get there first. Global Industries' motto? "Beating others to the bottom." To do that, they needed to lead the charge to develop the technology and equipment to go deeper. Few see a construction company as technology driven, but Global Industries became one so they could go where no one had gone before. Their methods and equipment are highly specialized and substantially developed in-house. They created methods and equipment for divers to go deeper and stay longer. For depths beyond 1,500 feet, where divers cannot go, they purchased mechanical robots that could do the work in up to 8,000 feet of water. Global Industries has put together the biggest multipurpose construction barge fleet in the world. These barges are more than floating platforms. They carry some of the biggest cranes in the world, can house more than two hundred workers, and carry a variety of sophisticated welding, pipe-spooling, and diving equipment. Barges designed for deep water no longer rely on anchors for exact positioning to lay pipe on the ocean floor but on GPS that controls thrusters on the barge's hull. Most barges are larger than a football field and contain innumerable innovations not only to rise to the challenge of going deeper, but also to provide the competitive advantage Global Industries has today. With Doré at the helm, Global Industries's attitude is that there is no obstacle that cannot be overcome by innovation.

Doré's Skill to Lead No. 3: Visionary

Early in his career, someone asked Doré what his long-term goal for Global Industries was. Without hesitation he answered, "I want to make Global the largest offshore construction company in the Gulf of Mexico." Perhaps every company has ambitious goals. But it's one thing to articulate an ambitious goal and another thing to have a constant vision of how to get there. The vision is not just of what one can become, but of one's industry, customers, and competitors.

Doré has a reputation as a man with a crystal ball who can read the trends of the industry better than anyone else. He is a continuous and tireless thinker. The 1970s were boom years for oil companies and related services, and this continued into the early 1980s. In 1981, Doré started to pick up numerous clues of an impending oil bust and started to prepare Global Industries for it, while other companies in the industry continued to pour in huge investments. He advised employees to get ready for hard times, told them not to buy houses or cars, and to save their money. The first effects of the recession were not felt until 1983, but Doré and Global Industries were then well positioned for his next vision: They took advantage of creative opportunities to acquire equipment and experienced workers to put Global Industries into the major league of full-service offshore construction companies. In the winter of 1985–86, as Global Industries kept its head above water, companies folded right and left. The late 1980s offered the biggest clearance sale in the history of oil and gas. Doré believed business would come back, and it was now all about in-stilling confidence to take advantage of the fire sale and prepare for a different future. From 1985 to 1992, Global Industries ac-quired numerous assets, many of them large and very specialized construction barges, some for less than ten cents on the dollar.

These were fantastic acquisitions, but all this new equip-ment required a different vision. Most of the equipment was highly specialized, not built with the versatility that Global In-dustries needed. Global Industries would have to retrofit the equipment, which would cost the company far more than the initial purchase. Doré, however, saw the equipment as diamonds in the rough. He had visions of what the barges *could* be, what they could do for the company, and the future work they could perform consistent with his vision of needing a nimble and ver-satile fleet. Doré's audacious visions brought Global Industries from small niche player to industry leader.

The Parlay

Both Christopher and Doré were able to parlay small sums and modest beginnings into highly lucrative, world-class organiza-tions. Christopher started a business with $3,000 and took it to sales of $700 million and 1,000 employees. Doré initially in-vested $8,000 in a business and took it to a value of more than $2.5 billion and 3,000 employees. The difference for each was taking their physical and cognitive work ethics and adding the skill of leadership. When they started, in addition to having the necessary physical and cognitive work ethics, their key skills looked something like this:

Initial Skill Sets

Doris Christopher	Bill Doré
Cooking expertise	Sales ability
Teaching	Teaching
Knowledge of home entertainment and hospitality	Coaching

They each then developed the unique leadership skills that allowed them to multiply their efforts.

Developed Leadership Skill Sets

Doris Christopher	Bill Doré
Culture creator and perpetrator	Team coaching
People selection	Innovation
Motivation	Team visionary

With well-developed physical and cognitive work ethics, Doris Christopher and Bill Doré got businesses off the ground. Then, when the demands of growing businesses made it necessary to conduct introspection on their work character in order that they grow as their companies did, they realized the missing component was skills to lead. They determined what skills to lead were necessary to their particular businesses and put them to work. In the end, they took businesses they'd made from scratch to the kind of success people dream about.

The Adversity Paradox Takeaways:
Putting Work Character to Work

- Work character is a broader concept than work ethic. Work character consists of one's physical work ethic, one's cognitive work ethic, and one's particular skills to lead.

• Using the diagnostic skill of introspection, assess your competency in each of these three parts of work character. Are you working and thinking as effectively as you need to be to attain your goals? What are your particular skills to lead? Do you have the right skills in place to perform well and to advance to the next level?

• Again using introspection, determine your main motivating factors for pursuing your particular career and in how well you perform on a day-to-day basis. Is your job just a job, just a means to an end? Or do you work for some higher, more fulfilling purpose? These are two poles on a continuum: Where do you fall? If you find yourself too close to the "job is just a job" end of the spectrum, what can you do to move in the opposite direction?

• Determine which of the suggested methods for improving your performance and attaining a more fulfilling career are right for you: the right motivation, visualization, "and then some," successful habits. Often, it is some combination of these. Right now, make a list of work character goals for the next six months and write down which of the suggested methods for improvement would be most beneficial in strengthening your weakness. Make a commitment to reaching those goals and then some, and not only will your overall work character and job performance improve, we bet you'll find that work will quickly become more fulfilling. Your new skills and increased motivation may even lead you into the position you've always dreamed of.

7

Purpose and Passion—You Really Can Take the Work Out of Work: *Human Capital Component No. 4*

The Purpose and Passion Advantage

"I skip to work," Warren Buffett famously said. Lee Iacocca said, "I love cars. I couldn't wait to get to work in the morning." For those who have found work they love, work is not work. And with Americans spending one-third of their lives at work and 70 percent of workers reporting dissatisfaction with their current jobs, finding work that is exciting is paramount. Anxiety and great trepidation on Sunday nights as a prelude to Monday mornings is hardly a desirable lifestyle. Most business leaders understand the high cost of unhappy workers, both to the employees and the company. The unhappy workers normally do just "enough to get by" while the happy workers routinely perform at the top of their game "and then some," and the difference in productivity is enormous. Have you ever met a successful person who wasn't passionate about what made her a success? And could you imagine the productivity of a company where everyone came to work with attitudes like Buffett's or Ia-cocca's?

Recognizing the importance of the connection between purpose and passion, businesses try to foster corporate statements that help develop and engage employee passion. The business leaders who get their mission statements right are the ones who know how to align purpose and passion. Wal-Mart's mission is "To give ordinary folk the chance to buy the same thing as rich people" and 3M's is "To solve unsolved problems innovatively." For years Microsoft has had a stated mission of "A computer on every desktop and in every home, running Microsoft software." It's very simple, focused, and easy to understand. Did these mission statements work? Did they foster and cultivate employee passion? The answer is in the results. So many "ordinary folk" purchase Wal-Mart's goods that it's become one of the most profitable businesses in America. 3M is in the Fortune 500 and has more than $24 billion in annual revenues. While there may not literally be a Microsoft system running in every home in America, it's safe to say that every household in America knows of Microsoft's staggering success. Clearly, the employees of these extremely successful companies are able to get passionate about the purpose of their work. The true measure of a stated business purpose is its ability to get its employees excited and engaged.

Let's look a little more closely at exactly what we mean by purpose and passion. Purpose is your life's highest calling. Quintessentially lofty goals such as finding a cure for cancer, working to end poverty, or striving to end the current climate crisis may easily come to mind, but purpose need not be so dramatic or enacted on such a grand scale. True purpose, no matter where it is found or how modest it may seem from the outside, is immeasurably powerful. Dr. Martin Luther King Jr. may have said it best: "If it falls your lot to be a street sweeper, sweep streets like Michelangelo painted pictures, like Shakespeare wrote poetry, like Beethoven composed music; sweep streets so well that all the host of Heaven and earth will have to pause to say, 'Here lived a great street sweeper, who swept his job well.'" The fact is, purpose can be found in any occupation. Providing clients with security and peace of mind may be a life insurance sales representative's purpose. Designing the world's most beautiful and innovative buildings may be an architect's purpose. Improving the quality of customers' lives may be the purpose of a pharmacist. Bringing quality products or services to consumers at affordable prices may be the purpose of the small business owner. Having the right purpose, the purpose that specifically works for you and your business, is central to creating passion that impacts results.

Passion is much less tangible. It's all about emotion and excitement. At its height it's almost magical. With sufficient passion, work is not the daily grind but something to look forward to with eager anticipation. But here's how purpose and passion align: Passion is the enthusiasm you feel as a result of your purpose. Your purpose generates your passion. It's the excitement the life insurance sales representative feels about selling a policy and the elation she feels because she's changed someone's life by giving them the comfort of security. It's the enthusiasm the architect displays throughout the design of a project and, upon completion, the great pride he takes in his accomplishment. It's the satisfaction the pharmacist feels in getting to know her customers and coaching them on the use of prescriptions, the joy she experiences in enhancing the quality of lives. It's the rewarding sense of a job well done and the pleasure of providing a good to the community the small business owner feels—not to mention the satisfaction of running a business on his own terms. Those who are able to find passion in their purpose enjoy increased productivity, confidence, and perseverance and an ability to envision a future with more possibilities. Finding passion in your work doesn't mean everything is perfect, but it means you have the ability and vision to see beyond the imperfections.

All this talk about purpose and passion begs an obvious question: Which came first? That is, did the successful people we studied find a passion and then align a purpose, or did they find a purpose and become passionate about it? Conventional wisdom tells us over and over that passion comes first, that it, in fact, finds you. But we think that's dead wrong. Yes, all those commencement addresses and motivational speeches have it exactly backward. You find purpose, and if it's the right purpose, passion follows.

And if it doesn't, you should keep looking for a purpose.

Solving World Hunger—a Pipe Dream?

How many times have you heard someone dismiss a difficult task by saying, "Forget it, it would be easier to solve world hunger"? It was a frequent refrain when we were growing up. Commercials featuring celebrities asking for donations to hunger relief bore images of emaciated children with bellies bloated from malnutrition, so weak they were unable to stand or even sit unassisted. In the 1960s and beyond, the pessimists outnumbered the optimists, and with good reason—the world's population was growing much faster than its food production, and people in all parts of the globe were starving.

But today, though insufficient food continues to be a problem in some areas, wide-scale world hunger is no longer the doomsday scenario it used to be. What happened to change this seemingly insurmountable problem?

A purpose in perfect alignment with passion had a lot to do with it.

There are five people who have received the Congressional Gold Medal, the Nobel Peace Prize, and the Presidential Medal of Freedom. They are Martin Luther King Jr., Mother Teresa, Elie Wiesel, Nelson Mandela, and, most recently, a man from small-town America by the name of Norman Borlaug. Borlaug's purpose in life was to accomplish what everyone said was impossible: solving world hunger. But certainly Borlaug wasn't born with this purpose. His life, like that of so many others, took some turns before he found the purpose that made him passionate enough to fully exploit his potential.

Borlaug grew up on a 130-acre farm. Through the eighth grade he attended the local school, a one-room schoolhouse with one teacher. The restrooms were outhouses. His teacher encouraged him to pursue high school, saying, "He's no great shakes as a scholar; his arithmetic is awful—but he sticks to it. He's got grit! High school will make him." In high school Borlaug was an athlete, and his ambition was to be a high school science teacher and coach. After high school he went to the University of Minnesota, where he planned to enroll in the College of Agriculture.

It was 1933 and the United States was at the bottom of the Great Depression. Borlaug was immediately troubled by the human misery he witnessed in the city, the likes of which he had never seen before. "Back on the farm," he said, "despite the Depression, bank failures, and farm foreclosures, we nearly always had plenty of food. But here in the city where people depend on a cash economy there is both hunger for food and hunger for work."

To get into the College of Agriculture Borlaug had to take an entrance exam, and it was a rude awakening to discover that his prior schooling had prepared him for it poorly. He failed the exam but was allowed to enroll in the General College at the University, which was geared toward students earning two-year associate degrees. The embarrassing failure and the new plan did not sit well with Borlaug, and it would serve as an adversity that motivated him. He worked hard to achieve decent grades at the General College, and after a couple of quarters he persuaded the university to let him transfer into the College of Agriculture to major in forestry.

His last summer before graduation, he landed a job with the U.S. Forest Service as a lookout in the Idaho National Forest. This would lead to a job offer as a full-time assistant ranger after he completed his bachelor's degree in 1937, which he accepted. But before he even graduated, the job was eliminated due to budget cuts. With the encouragement of his new wife, Margaret, he decided to stay in school and do postgraduate work. He also attended a very inspiring and timely lecture by University of Minnesota professor E. C. Stakman on plant pathology. Stakman would soon become a mentor, and Borlaug moved from forest pathology to plant pathology, an area of study that Stakman suggested could provide him with more options down the road. He stuck with it, earning a master's degree in 1940 and a doctorate in 1941. His studies complete, he took a job with DuPont in Wilmington, Delaware.

Borlaug's purpose emerged after his second year at DuPont.

Professor Stakman had gone to work for the Rockefeller Foundation, which had a mission to "promote the well-being of mankind throughout the world." They wanted to hire Borlaug as part of a team of scientists to go to Mexico. The Rockefeller Foundation had been working in Mexico for about twenty years as part of a cooperative public health program. With the cooperation of the Mexican government and the encouragement of the U.S. government, they were looking to shift their emphasis to food production, closer to the root cause of both social and health problems. Sold on the challenge of conquering hunger in Mexico, Borlaug took the job.

In late 1944 he moved to Mexico, never having been there and unable to speak a word of Spanish. Living and work conditions were miserable. Early progress was slow and arduous. Borlaug often spent the hours from dawn to dusk crossbreeding wheat with surgical-type tweezers, tending the experimental fields, and studying and detailing each new variety of wheat. By 1952 he had entries for 6,000 individual crosses of wheat, and a handful showing promise.

Conventional wisdom at the time was to breed crops in the area where they would be grown, one crop, one round of breeding, per year. But Borlaug came up with an innovative technique. By working in two different latitudes in Mexico he was able to double the amount of breeding, shuttling seeds back and forth to get two growing seasons within a given year. The process, called shuttle-breeding, was initially frowned upon by the head of the program. But Borlaug was convinced the project would fail without shuttle-breeding, and he resigned over the matter. Fortunately, Professor Stakman intervened. Shuttle-breeding was approved, and Borlaug agreed to stay on. By 1956 Borlaug, by crossing varieties of Mexican wheat with wheat from around the world, had developed forty new varieties of wheat, and Mexico was self-sufficient in wheat production. By 1961 he had developed a shorter, more robust, and disease-resistant dwarf Mexican wheat. The 1963 harvest was six times larger than the 1944 harvest, the year Borlaug arrived.

From Mexico, Borlaug took the new dwarf Mexican wheat and introduced varieties into Pakistan and India. There yields nearly doubled between 1965 and 1970. Pakistan became self-sufficient in 1968 and India self-sufficient in 1974. The collective increases in yield were labeled the Green Revolution, and Borlaug is often credited with having saved more than a billion people from starvation.

Stop and think about that for a moment. A *billion* lives. One billion people saved from starvation because Norman Borlaug found a purpose he was extremely passionate about. This is an extreme example of the extraordinary results that can be achieved when one aligns purpose and passion. Borlaug doesn't operate in the traditional world of business, but his contributions are too great to ignore. He provides the perfect model of what can be achieved when one has found the right purpose and is passionate about it.

We're not the only ones who think so. We asked a close friend of Borlaug's, former ambassador to Cambodia and president of the World Food Prize, Kenneth Quinn, what he thought of Borlaug's pursuit of purpose and passion. "Norman is ninety-three now and remains very determined to combat world hunger—he's still got a lengthy punch list of things left to do," Quinn said. "His passion has paid huge dividends for society, but if passion had been the only driver in his life he would be in pursuit of trying to be the Chicago Cubs second baseman." Passion is absolutely necessary, and workers who are passionate about their purposes are incredibly motivated. But it's *purpose* that drives that passion. Purpose will last a lifetime, while passion ebbs and wanes. Find your true purpose, and passion will follow. Find your true purpose, and you've found the way not only to take the work out of work, but also to contribute to society in a lasting, meaningful way.

Now, how about purpose in the arena of business? What happens when someone pursues a purpose found in business with the same passion with which Borlaug assuaged world hunger?

Clay Jones: Take Serendipity and Run with It

There is no single tried-and-true way to find one's purpose. Borlaug's purpose veritably announced itself to him when he encountered a problem big enough that it could not be ignored, a problem he was uniquely qualified to combat. But few people find their purpose this way, and even fewer know their purpose from very early on. The far more common scenario is one of gaining a certain amount of life experience—perhaps with no small amount of trial and error—before one is able to discern a purpose worthy of a life's work. We'd like to introduce you to two business professionals whose journeys to discover their purposes took vastly different turns.

Clay Jones is the president and CEO of Rockwell Collins. Rockwell Collins, founded in 1933, is a company engaged in the design, production, and support of communications and aviation electronics worldwide. It is a leading designer and manufacturer of everything from missile guidance systems to in-flight entertainment systems for commercial airlines, and is the U.S. Army's leading provider of handheld global positioning systems. Their products can be seen in use with the space shuttle and military and commercial aircraft.

Jones has been at the helm since 2001, and there's no question that he has led the company to great success. He took Rockwell public just months before 9/11, and then guided it successfully through the huge losses in commercial business the industry faced following 9/11. In 2004, *Forbes* magazine selected Rockwell as the best-managed aerospace and defense company in America. In 2007 it was selected for the Business-Week 50, an elite group of S&P 500 companies that represent the best in class.

Jones is one of the lucky ones. He's living out his purpose—to work in the aviation industry—and the passion he feels for aviation, Rockwell Collins, his employees, and the customers Rockwell serves is palpable within minutes of meeting him. His knowledge of aviation isn't just theoretical, either, and it isn't just about the bottom line: A former pilot with the U.S. Air Force, he's logged thousands of hours of flight time all over the world. Based on the man he is today, one would guess that he was the kid whose room was filled with model airplanes and who dreamed of flying. Accordingly, we asked Jones if he had an early passion for flying, an early inkling that being a pilot was his purpose. His answer was unequivocal: "Absolutely not."

"In fact," he said, laughing, "the irony of that is, my cousin was that kid. He and his family lived in the neighborhood and all my life I can remember him being passionate about airplanes. He wore bomber jackets, and he made model airplanes that he hung all over his room. I hung around him a lot and saw his passion all the time, and I also had a father who was a navigator in World War II. He flew twenty-three missions over Europe in a B-24, was shot down, and spent 401 days as a POW. Later on, he was a reservist in the air force. And still, with all that influencing me, I wasn't passionate about flying, not at all."

So how, we asked, did he get from zero interest in flying to a career in aviation and becoming a leader of one of the most recognized aerospace companies in the world?

"Serendipity," he said.

Serendipity? Noticing our quizzical looks, he went on to elaborate. First, he was quick to point out that by serendipity he doesn't mean simple luck. Serendipity isn't a matter of being at the right place at the right time or buying the winning lottery ticket. Rather, the Jones application of serendipity is about encountering the numerous forks in the road of life—most of which are entirely unforeseen and many of which come about through no conscious choice of our own—and then making a conscious choice to pursue a direction with vigor and perseverance. "You find yourself in certain positions in life where you have to make a decision," he said, "and the fact is, each of these decisions has a profound effect on your future direction in life, which is something most of us underappreciate at the time. Looking back, I know now that the vast majority of life is serendipity—each of those decisions builds upon a new direction, a direction we never could've foreseen. And that," he said, "is how I eventually found my purpose. One thing led to another—and sometimes I wasn't happy with the immediate outcome of the choices I made—but I stuck to it and pursued every new direction with everything I had. I may not have been sure of what was coming next, and every now and again I second-guessed myself, but I aspired to do well at everything."

And there is the difference between a lucky break that just happens to lead to a new opportunity and the kind of serendipity Jones is talking about. Nothing fell into his lap, and he wasn't a passive bystander accepting what "fate" threw his way; rather, he conducted some good introspection, made conscious choices, worked extremely hard at whatever direction he'd chosen, and made the most of every new opportunity.

To see Jones's idea of serendipity in action, let's rewind for a moment and look at his full life story. Clay Jones was born in 1949 in Nashville, Tennessee, the son of a schoolteacher and a homemaker. "I came from a mixed working-class neighborhood, and staying there would have been fine, a good life," he said, "but I had aspirations to be more than what I saw around me." His father had come from a tough life and modest means, and his schoolteacher's salary didn't stretch very far; Jones said he can't remember his father ever having fewer than two jobs, and sometimes it was three. Both his parents ingrained in him the value of education and how it could be an avenue for increasing the quality of his life, so he worked hard to get good grades. He found himself grouped with other high-achieving students, and the association had a positive effect, inspiring him to achieve even more. "I fed off those kids," he said. "They were bright and wanted to do something significant with their lives."

Another extremely positive influence—one that would prove to be one of those serendipitous events that shaped Jones's future—was taking on leadership positions. In fact, he describes his early experience in leadership as one of the most important formative events in setting the direction of his life. "I was active in a number of clubs and activities," he said, "and then I ran for student body president and won. I got a taste for leadership, and it tasted pretty good! I enjoyed being out front, and there seemed to be a natural fit. So, early on I developed an aspiration to be a leader, and it's carried over through the rest of my life." Jones continued his aspirations for leadership in college by becoming involved in student ambassadors and student senate.

Another serendipitous event that became a defining moment for Jones was one of those things he had no control over: the draft. "The Vietnam War was still going hot and heavy in 1967," he said, "and most people were finding their way into the military one way or another, and most of those were finding their way to Vietnam." Knowing that the same would be true for him, Jones's father suggested that he join ROTC so he could enter the military as an officer; he also encouraged Jones to enter the air force. Jones describes his father's experience and guidance as pivotal for him, and indeed that was the case: After his first year in ROTC, he earned a scholarship that underwrote the cost of his next three years of college. "That scholarship was huge for me," Jones said, "because to pay tuition I'd been relying on my summer job mowing lawns and whatever my parents could give me."

It's just these sorts of eventualities that Jones is talking about when he speaks of serendipity. "Those two things," he said—his early aspiration for leadership and joining the ROTC—"were the key factors for directing me in the rest of my life. They got me into working in aerospace and what eventually led to my purpose in the aviation industry and my adult career. It was serendipity how I ended up in ROTC, the air force, and then taking the pilot's exam." In ROTC Jones, like everyone else, was given the opportunity to take the pilot's exam. Those who did well would be pilot-qualified upon graduation. He may not have been passionate about aviation then, but he was passionate about doing well at whatever was placed in front of him. So one thing followed another: The possibility of serving in Vietnam led him to ROTC, ROTC led to the pilot's exam, scoring well on the exam led him to pilot training, which led him to the air force and flight school, all of which served to help Jones discover his purpose.

But it would be years before Jones arrived at that point. We were fascinated to learn that although Jones immediately took to his leadership role in the air force—at twenty-two he was flying an F-4 Phantom, a supersonic fighter-bomber, and was responsible for a group of younger airmen—his first experiences with flying were anything but pleasurable, and a passion for flying was a remote possibility at best. He vividly remembers his first few jet flights—the smell of jet fuel, the claustrophobic feel in a helmet and mask, the suffocating heat, and pulling Gs all while the instructor pilot squawked orders in his ear. And the nausea. "After landing those first few flights I was just green and completely without my equilibrium," he said. "I remember saying to myself, 'Why would anyone want to do this?'" But true to form, Jones didn't give up. "It wasn't fun. In fact, it was downright uncomfortable, but like everything in life, you start to develop a taste for it. Soon enough I got acclimated, and the physical discomfort of flying started to dissipate, and I could see through the momentary drudgery to the thrill of what I was doing, the beauty of flight and the exhilaration of it. All of a sudden, flying began to get fun. And that," Jones said, "was the way my whole career in aviation transitioned." Even after ROTC, even after flight training, and especially after his first flights, he still didn't have a passion for flying, and certainly didn't see a purpose there. But he wanted to succeed, and once he'd decided to pursue something, he was not one to give up.

Jones's explanation of how he came to love flying, which was no easy task, makes a very prominent point about the role of serendipity in his life, and about relying on "and then some" to persevere through a difficult situation. "I did not always do what I wanted to do, but once I got past the unpleasantness I really liked what I was doing," he said. "The more I flew, the more I liked it, and at a certain point I realized that I was doing something that very few human beings get the opportunity to do. I began to get the sensory exhilaration of it all, the challenge of it, and the thrill of survival, knowing the outcome to not performing well is death, both in combat and out. Once I realized all the possibilities and opportunities of flying, I realized a purpose may be there. At first, I didn't know that aviation was where my purpose lay because at that early point, I just didn't know what it was about. But I stuck around and I learned, and to this day I'd say I'm very passionate about aviation and flight and the difficulty and complexity not only of the aircraft's systems but of the organizations that are doing it."

From 1971 to 1979 Jones had a career in the air force most would envy. Not only was he flying the F-4, but in 1976 he received a prestigious new aircraft assignment with the new F-15 and its very first operational fighter wing. Though he'd entered the air force under the assumption that he'd serve in Vietnam, by this time the war was winding down, and another set of opportunities in different parts of the globe appeared. Over eight years Jones was stationed in six different places, and for a kid who'd hardly been outside of Tennessee, seeing the world was a big deal. There were stints in Texas, Florida, and Virginia and overseas assignments in England and South Korea. He got the chance to show off the relatively new F-15 in such places as Saudi Arabia, Sudan, South Korea, and the Philippines. By this time Jones's passion was alive and well, and he had decided that life in the air force was where he would serve until retirement.

But the air force was going through a number of changes. There was backlash from the Vietnam War, and American military personnel were not revered by the public as they had been in the past. The Carter administration was also making deep military cuts that affected both equipment and personnel. Jones saw some of the best airplanes in the world grounded while awaiting spare parts. Compounding the situation was inflation: Air force pay increases were running one-third to one-half of inflation. Jones believes he could have survived all that—when you're passionate about something, what amounts to a major obstacle for most is a mere nuisance—but a host of people he greatly admired were leaving the air force for greener pastures. The commercial airlines were hiring like crazy and were paying two and three times the salaries of the air force. They were requiring just seventy-five hours of work a month, much less than the air force, which would allow Jones time to pursue his interest in business.

In the end, Jones made the difficult decision to leave the air force, intending to sign on with a commercial airline. He reasoned that he could still live out his purpose in flying and keep his passions alive. He also thought the career move might create other opportunities, such as getting into leadership via a management position or maybe even having enough time and money someday to start his own business. Then, as Jones put it, "serendipity struck again." In late 1979 there was an oil crisis and the cost of fuel skyrocketed. Seemingly overnight, the airlines went into a slump and stopped hiring. With his departure from the air force already set, Jones realized he'd made the mistake of putting all his eggs in one basket.

While soul-searching on what to do next, he ran across a former flight commander with whom he'd served in South Korea, who told him that Rockwell was looking to fill a marketing position in Southern California. Not having a plan B, Jones jumped at the opportunity, fit or no fit, and signed on with Rockwell Collins. What happened next probably seemed like a cruel irony: Literally one week after starting at Rockwell, Delta Air Lines called and offered him a piloting job. "I'm sitting there thinking, 'What have I done?'" Jones said. "Why has life thrown me this curveball?" But as Jones had committed himself to Rockwell, he felt obligated to decline Delta's offer, which shocked the Delta Air Lines representative— no one had ever turned down their offer before.

He'd done the honorable thing, but that didn't mean he didn't sometimes second-guess himself. In fact, he was "miserable" his first eight months at Rockwell, and more than once wondered if he'd made a terrible mistake—adversity he didn't at all expect. "Having no expertise on the technical equipment Rockwell was developing or the military acquisition process my new job required, I was unable to make any meaningful contribution," he said. "I was lost in the wilderness." But he had strong introspection skills to pull him through the difficulty. And having had the experience of persevering through the early days of flying and eventually coming to love it, even to the point of finding his purpose there, he had a strong belief in serendipity. He knew that if he stuck with Rockwell, something good would come of it. On the other side of the coin, he also knew he didn't have to lie back and simply "grin and bear it" through the unpleasantness; he knew he needed to take action.

He started networking with other parts of Rockwell. One was a division that had been heavily invested in the canceled B-1A bomber program. Striving to replace canceled work, the division was going after smaller contracts and attempting to get into the tactical fighter business. Jones realized their objective was a much better fit, given his interests and experience and his time in a fighter cockpit, and he moved into that division. After a year of wandering and wondering, he was back in more familiar territory and starting to feel better about what he was doing. The passion he had felt in high school and college for leadership and then later as a pilot was starting to glimmer again, and this time it was directed toward aviation and the company he worked for.

Serendipity then struck again two years later. His supervisor recommended that he get some direct sales and marketing experience, and as it happened, he had a chance to go into the President's Commission on Executive Exchange program for a year. So Jones moved to Washington D.C., and then ended up staying because Reagan had been elected and had promised to restore the B-1 program. In the end, he remained in Washington for another twelve years and moved up through the management ranks of Rockwell. He eventually became president of the Washington office, and when the head of the D.C. office retired, Jones moved into that position. "All my passions came together at one time," he said, "leadership, aerospace, and working in the political arena—yes, I even got to use my undergrad degree in political science!"

Since then Jones has held several positions of prominence

with Rockwell. In 2001 he was named president and CEO, and a year later, chairman. As a result of working hard, not giving up in the face of adversity, and being open to unexpected opportunities, Jones finds himself working within the enviable nexus of all his passions and living out his life's purpose. He's living and enjoying the fruits of serendipity.

A few rare people may know their purpose very early on, but for most of us, there's a certain amount of trial and error involved, a certain amount of trying things out until we find the right fit. This was certainly the case for Clay Jones's path, and his story reveals an unexpected truth: Your purpose may not always be what you want or think it should be, at least not at first. Your purpose actually may not become clear until you make some firm decisions and take some concrete actions. Because Jones persevered in every eventuality life threw his way and aspired to succeed in every endeavor, he "accidentally"—or, as he would say, "serendipitously"—discovered his purpose. This is how Jones found a purpose he became passionate about—passion so strong it took the work out of work. His story teaches us that we should be open to unexpected opportunities and that we need to give every new opportunity an honest chance. Never underestimate the profound effect that decisions you make now could have on your future, and if you strive to do well at every endeavor and at every juncture and stick it out through any short-term unpleasantness, you can expect to achieve great results. "That's the game, isn't it," said Jones. "You do well and you get more, and better, options." What may look like luck on the surface is actually the result of your hard work and your ability to make the most of whatever life throws your way.

Walter Scott Jr.: The Evolution of One's Purpose and Passion

Throughout our careers we've come across plenty of people who at one time were very excited and passionate about what they were doing but had lost the fire inside of them. Whether it was disillusionment for some reason, plateauing, or contentment, people go off soul-searching from time to time. The most commonly heard phrase signifying the loss of passion is "I'm bored at my job." A cursory glance at today's hiring trends indicates that waning passion is more common than not. A 2007 CNNMoney poll of more than 11,000 people revealed that nearly half of the respondents were thinking of changing jobs soon. A study conducted by the U.S. Bureau of Labor Statistics revealed that on average, the youngest of the baby boomers held 10.5 jobs between the ages of eighteen and forty, and young workers today fully expect to switch jobs several or even many times in their lifetimes. The days of signing on with one company and retiring from there are long gone.

We're all for job changes that advance one's career, but a résumé that reflects a dozen or more jobs in just as many years would be a red flag to any employer—and, we would add, is a clear indication of someone who has not yet found his or her purpose. To better understand how one avoids getting bored at a job and keeps the fire lit we interviewed one of the most successful and passionate people we know, Walter Scott Jr. Scott, unlike most of those in today's workforce, has remained with the same company his entire career.

Scott is listed by *Forbes* magazine as one of the four hundred richest people in America, with a net worth in excess of $1.8 billion. He served as CEO and president of Peter Kiewit Sons', Inc. for nineteen years and currently serves as a director of Berkshire Hathaway, Level 3 Communications, MidAmerican Energy Holdings, Valmont Industries, and Peter Kiewit Sons', Inc. He has been featured in numerous publications, including *Forbes, USA Today,* and *Barron's.* Let's take a look at his career trajectory to see how he found his purpose—or, as you'll see, purposes—and how he sustained a high level of passion for so many years.

Born in 1931 during the Great Depression, Scott developed his physical work ethic while still very young, shoveling snow for neighbors when he was only eight and then working summers on farms and ranches in his teens. His parents instilled in him the value of education and the need to have a degree. He left his home town of Omaha, Nebraska (where he met a young Warren Buffett, with whom he is still friends), to attend college at Colorado A&M, now Colorado State. His intention was to get a degree in range management, a subject that intrigued him, given his summer work. When he arrived at A&M he came across an acquaintance, an older student who was in the engineering program. He suggested that an engineering degree would be of more value to Scott. "He told me that it would be a tougher course than what I was thinking about, and that it would teach me to think logically," Scott said. "He also said it would provide me with a background to do just about anything I wanted. This man was very smart, and I had a lot of respect for him, so guess what—I signed up for civil engineering." Scott now marvels at the direction it took him. "What seemed like such an insignificant incident at the time had a huge impact on my life." Clay Jones would describe this as one of life's serendipitous moments. And like Jones, Scott's college involvement in ROTC would unwittingly pave the way for the next step on his journey.

Now old enough to work in construction, Scott returned from college each summer to work for Kiewit. Money was tight, and as we saw with a number of our profiles, Scott worked from the day school let out for the summer to the day before school started in the fall, earning as much money as possible. After graduating with his engineering degree, he still had almost no idea of what his purpose would be, and without a purpose, he wasn't yet passionate about anything. With little idea of what to do next, Scott worked for a short time for Kiewit, then followed the standard practice of the day and signed up for military duty. "Back then," Scott said, "if you were in ROTC you just ended up going into the military. I went into the air force and signed on for a two-year stint."

At that time the United States was involved in the Korean War. Scott was enthusiastic about serving his country, but he knew from the beginning that a military career wasn't where his purpose lay. "I entered as a second lieutenant and left as a second lieutenant," Scott said. "That's as low as you can get. I fulfilled my duties, but it's safe to say I wasn't passionate about military service." He was in material services command, which organized and shipped supplies to soldiers in Korea. It was a worthwhile cause, but Scott was given no responsibility or authority, and thus felt his work had little meaning. If there was ever a time when he found himself bored and unchallenged, this was it. "During that time," he said, "if I could muster up any passion at all, I would get myself organized to go fishing." Scott put in his two years and left.

He went back to what he knew and enjoyed: Kiewit, his old summer employer. They had seen his work ethic, and now that he had an engineering diploma in hand and two years of military experience, they didn't hesitate to hire him as an engineer. By this time Scott had a wife and child. His first assignment was a big one: construction of the Monticello Dam in Northern California, which would rise to be more than thirty stories tall. The Scott family packed everything they owned into their car and a single-wheel trailer and headed west.

To his delight, Scott found the work extremely rewarding, and he described the contracting business in general as "very satisfying." "You've got a job that can be completed in a reasonable time frame, a job with a beginning, middle, and end," he said. "So you have the chance to see it happen from start to finish—getting a project organized, getting it going, and even getting a chance to make and correct your mistakes. At the end of the project, you can look at what you've accomplished and say, 'I was a part of that, and what we built added some long-term value or service to society.'" The Monticello Dam, for instance, is still supplying power and flood control all these years later. Scott also cites the U.S. road system as another prime example. Kiewit built more miles of the U.S. Interstate Highway System than any other contractor. "The value to society our interstate system provides is inestimable," he said. "Think of what this country would be today if we didn't have an interstate system."

Happily, Scott found himself in the exact opposite situation of his time in the military. He had great responsibilities, authority over projects, and best of all, he could see that his contributions were providing immense value to society. His work was both rewarding and worthwhile, not in the least onerous or unchallenging. In other words, Scott was beginning to see his purpose—to build infrastructures that improved society—and the passion he felt for doing so indicated he was on the right track.

For his next project he packed up the family and headed east to work on the Saint Lawrence Seaway, the second of seventeen project moves he would make with his family over a twelve-year period. The seaway is a series of dams, locks, and canals that permit oceangoing vessels to travel between the Atlantic and the Great Lakes. At the time of construction it was considered to be the largest work of engineering of all time. All the moves with his family were not easy, but they came with the territory and Scott was prepared for it. "As the work does not come to us," he said, "we go to where the work is." For those who are passionate about what they are doing the price paid to play never seems too high.

With all the moves, the hard work, and the experience he gained, Scott steadily worked his way up the ladder at Kiewit, but in spite of the advancement he found that he wanted more. He also believed he was fully capable of even greater responsibilities. "Setting goals has always been something I've done," he said, "and one goal I had put out in front of me was to start my own company. My plan was to learn my job and everything else the best I could and within three years start my own company."

Meanwhile, Scott's desire and talent were not going unnoticed. The chairman and principal owner of Kiewit, Peter Kiewit, took notice of Scott's advancement and personally began mentoring him. He kept Scott challenged, never allowing him to become complacent or allowing the fire to wane. With every move, Kiewit gave Scott additional responsibilities and more stimulating work. The three-year window Scott had set himself for starting his own business kept moving as he was constantly being moved to a new and more challenging role, to bigger and more complicated projects to be built. "I think Peter did that to keep me challenged," Scott said. "And he did that up until his death in 1979, when I ended up running the company." Scott may never have started his own company, but he was now running one of the largest construction contractors in the world.

At the time Scott took over as CEO, Kiewit was principally a construction business with some mining interests. The company had been founded in 1884 and was a Nebraska general building contractor before Peter Kiewit, the second generation of the family to run the company and the majority owner, took Kiewit into infrastructure construction to survive the Great Depression. At the same time he began selling some stock to key managers, laying the foundation for what Kiewit would become. Company growth would come through construction projects that supported the war effort in the 1940s and the cold war buildup in the 1950s, and finally through their work on the interstate highway system. Kiewit became one of North America's largest transportation contractors, eventually dubbed "The Colossus of Roads" by *Forbes* magazine. Under Scott's leadership those businesses grew and prospered, and Kiewit became one of the leading heavy construction firms in the nation.

Kiewit is also one of the largest employee-owned firms in the nation, with more than 1,900 U.S. and Canadian employee shareholders. For Scott the employee ownership and the perpetual organization went hand in hand. "We have to look our owners in the face every day," he said. "Along with delivering superior results that positively impact society, there's no greater motivation for performing well." At present the company has about 6,000 salaried employees and 15,000 to 20,000 hourly employees. "We are 100 percent owned by active employees," Scott said. "If you're not active then you're out. It's quite a big deal. That is basically what had made us successful, that one basic thing. We make a market in the stock and guarantee we will buy, and they have to sell their stock." Another basic thing that has contributed to their success is a bit of wisdom Scott learned from his mentor. "From the beginning Peter didn't believe we needed to be the biggest, but we needed to be the best," he said. "I wholeheartedly subscribe to that philosophy. Our aim is to get work at the right price, build it in the most economical way, and conserve assets."

Clearly, the philosophy has worked. Kiewit has been extremely profitable, and its success created another issue—what do you do with extra money? It's one of those good problems to have. "If you run a contracting business the way we've been able to run Kiewit, you end up with more cash than you can use in the business," Scott explained. "So if you accumulate the cash and put it into, say, government bonds, then your people's returns go down. So I came to the conclusion that we needed to put that extra cash into starting new ventures, and our shareholders got the same number of shares in each company. This enabled Kiewit to retain the ability to get a good return."

Throughout the 1980s and 1990s Scott led Kiewit to invest its excess capital in everything from high-speed fiber-optic networks to public and private toll roads to geothermal power plants, and they've garnered superior returns. "Today we're in exactly the same shape," Scott said. "We have more equity and cash than needed to run the contracting business efficiently. We can diversify our investments and show the people who come in and work for us a record of high returns—we're still averaging 22 to 24 percent—and when they buy stock we can get them that kind of return." *Barron's* magazine deemed Scott "one of the shrewdest investors in the world."

Scott's career trajectory certainly shows a change in purpose, and this may be the key to how he remained at the same company for so long and why his passion never waned: His purpose, while firmly rooted in Kiewit and its concerns, evolved over the years. From building projects that positively impacted society to the stewardship of Kiewit and the well-being of its employee stockholders to investing in and starting other businesses, each step in Scott's evolving purpose built upon the next. And though Scott officially has retired from Kiewit, he remains extremely active in the company and its many successful ventures, one of which is Level 3 Communications, which operates one of the largest communications and Internet backbones in the world. "As far as I'm concerned," he said, "I haven't retired. I just don't have a permanent job." That's a true sign of a person who's found his life's purpose—or rather, purposes—and whose passion remains as fervent as ever.

More recently, Scott's purpose has come to encompass civic duty as well. He is chairman of Omaha's Henry Doorly Zoo and part owner of the Omaha Royals, a AAA baseball team. He has established an endowed fund at the University of Nebraska's Peter Kiewit Institute that each year provides more than 150 scholarships to high-achieving engineering and information technology students. "I'm particularly proud of our Scott Scholars," Scott said. "Over 90 percent graduate, they started their own alumni association, and this past year they raised $10,000 and put it back into the scholarship fund." In addition to the scholarships, Scott has built up a considerable infrastructure around the university's Peter Kiewit Institute. The Suzanne and Walter Scott Foundation has built a residence hall and conference center complex, ten apartment-style student housing buildings, a secure computing center, and a center for incubator and technical businesses.

In fact, Scott was passionate about so many things, we asked him what the underlying driver was. "I'm still passionate about infrastructure that adds great value to society," he said. "Look at MidAmerican Energy, for instance, one of our interests. Mid-American provides power and service to people all over the country. But the real passion for business overall comes from winning, and the only way to know if you've won or lost is to keep score. I think my pal Warren said that at some time or another," he said, smiling. "But it's absolutely true. In business you should win much more than 50 percent of the time, and it's absolutely important to me to keep score. I'd apply this to anything you attempt, actually, civic duties included. Whether you're trying to build things, provide things, increase membership, increase education, or what have you, all those things are measurable, and you need to measure your progress and make sure you're meeting your objectives.

"And winning," he said with a smile, "only increases your passion."

The Adversity Paradox Takeaways:
Finding a Purpose and Aligning Purpose and Passion

- Purpose comes first. Once you find your true purpose, passion will follow. Passion can be a great measure as to whether you've found your purpose or not: If passion never arrives, move on and try to find a different purpose.
- It may take time to discover a purpose. Stick with a task until you're sure that passion won't develop.
- Purpose may change over time.

- Purpose can be adjusted to fit circumstances.
- Which list more accurately describes your current work situation?

A

— Work is not work.

— Time at work flies by.

— Enthusiasm is common.

— "And them some" comes without a second thought.

B

— Work is drudgery.

— Doing only "enough to get by" is the norm.

— Your vision cannot get past the imperfections.

If the answer is B, can better framing or adjusting of your purpose increase your ability to become passionate and positively impact your success trajectory?

8

The Transformative Power
of a Lifelong Thirst for Knowledge:
Human Capital Component No. 5

Knowledge is power.
Nothing can stop the power of the enlightened mind.
Education is the best way to get ahead.
The only real mistake is the one from which we learn nothing.

The truth of these statements has been borne out across generations, cultures, and history. But could it be that the words have become so familiar that we've forgotten the power behind them? We could write a book on the value of education—and plenty of people have already done so—so here let us narrow our focus. What is the value of knowledge and education for the business-savvy professional?

We hardly know where to begin! Business-savvy professionals absolutely thrive on the thirst for knowledge. It's knowledge that enables you to formulate a vision and execute it successfully. It's knowledge that enables you to think on your feet, to act quickly and judiciously when problems or opportunities arise. It's knowledge that allows you to switch back and forth effortlessly from systems to linear thinking, from seeing the big picture to scrutinizing the details. It's knowledge that enables you to synthesize the mountains of data we all encounter each and every day into salient, useful information. It's knowledge that powers confident and effective leadership and inspires your team's confidence in you. When you know your stuff, your team trusts you implicitly. It's knowledge that enables you to select, train, and inspire business-savvy teams. It's even knowledge that allows you to see your *lack* of knowledge. The more you learn, the more you'll realize how much you don't know. And if you have the right knowledge skills and the means to learn, you'll know exactly how to fill those information voids.

So what is the source of this kind of knowledge? As far as we know, there are no classes in Systems Thinking 101, Foundations of Outstanding Visionary Skills, or Introduction to Knowing What You Do Not Know. The kind of knowledge we're talking about is firmly rooted in formal learning—the education we all received in the classroom—but is actually the product of *lifelong learning*. It comes as a result of gaining a keen thirst for knowledge one relentlessly tries to satisfy. And let us hasten to add that this unquenchable thirst, this ceaseless pursuit of knowledge, is anything but a burden: We're talking about an ongoing intellectual curiosity that drives business-savvy professionals to continually—and enthusiastically—discover and assimilate useful information. For people who've discovered a true thirst for knowledge, learning is a joy.

In this chapter we're going to look at the pivotal role education played in the lives of the business-savvy individuals we researched. We'll review how and when some of them discovered or acquired a lifelong thirst for knowledge, and introduce you to a business-savvy leader with one of the most amazing thirsts for knowledge we've ever encountered. It's our hope that these stories will lead you to discover, develop, and sustain your own thirst for knowledge. This fifth and final component of human capital alone has worked wonders in people's success trajectories, but added to the full business-savvy framework, it's guaranteed to transform not only your career but also your life.

Formal and Informal Learning

Let's begin by taking a brief look at how we learn and obtain knowledge. We can break the ways down into two broad categories—*formal* and *informal*. We're all familiar with formal learning: It's the learning that takes place within a structured teacher-student relationship. Grade school, high school, college, night-school classes, training seminars, and online courses are all examples of formal learning.

Informal, then, encompasses the balance of our learning. Much of informal learning results from what we do and experience in daily life. It's how we learned to speak, how we learned to play sports in the sandlot, or even how we learned to deal with a new gadget when we couldn't find the patience to read the instructions. Informal learning can involve a lot of trial and error. We learn through experience, by failing and succeeding. Unlike formal learning, with informal learning we have almost total control over the input to which we expose ourselves and which data we choose to synthesize. Boning up to buy a new car or home, researching which stocks to invest in, or reading *The Adversity Paradox* are all types of informal learning. Informal learning can also occur in social situations, and often when we're not even aware of accumulating knowledge: There's no telling what you can learn from a member of your breakfast club, during lunch with a colleague, or by being involved in organizations such as charities and church and civic groups.

The Palo Alto–based nonprofit Institute for Research on Learning reports that at least 80 percent of how people learn their jobs comes through informal means. Over a lifetime, most people spend far more time on and gain far more knowledge from informal learning. But while informal learning is clearly critical to success, we strongly believe that without the skills the formal learning environment provides, the informal learner has little chance of accumulating the quantity and quality of knowledge needed to gain business savvy and be successful.

The experiences of the members of our database bear this out. As part of our research for this book, we reviewed profiles of hundreds of successful individuals who overcame adversity at some point in their lives and compiled the profiles into a database of business-savvy leaders. We initially compiled our database giving no thought to educational levels. We were simply looking for people who had overcome adversity and now displayed incredible business savvy. Then, late in the writing of this book, when we did take a look at formal educational levels, here's what we discovered: 100 percent of our database had graduated from high school, 79 percent held at least a bachelor's degree, and 32 percent held a degree above a bachelor's. These are remarkably high numbers, but given that we're looking at a pool of overachievers, not surprising. What *is* surprising, and terribly sad, is the statistics for the country at large. The U.S. Census Bureau reveals that one in three Americans drops out of college, and according to the latest government figures *more than 50 percent* of college freshmen do not receive a degree within six years. For some minority groups, the numbers are much worse.

It's beyond this book's purview to diagnose why America's future leaders are dropping out of college in such alarming numbers, but what we can do is show you, through the lives of our database of business-savvy professionals, how vastly important a formal education is and give you a brief glimpse of what they gained from their formal education.

Our database's extraordinary high levels of formal education alone attest to how important they considered education. But what we discovered once we delved deeper than numbers makes an even stronger case. You may not be surprised to learn that these are people who pursued and gained their formal educations despite significant adversity.

Many of them, for example, simply didn't have the money to go to school, but knowing the high value of education, they found a way to get it. Richard Rosenberg, for example, retired chairman and CEO of Bank of America, came from a very poor family and paid his way through undergraduate school waiting tables every summer. Upon graduating he spent five years in the navy before using the GI Bill to finance a master's in business administration and a law degree. Joseph Pichler, retired CEO of the Kroger Co., can name twenty jobs he held while working his way through Notre Dame. John Mack, who for thirty years worked for Morgan Stanley and is now CEO there, is the son of Lebanese immigrants and started working when he was eight. His parents encouraged him to do well in school. He became a member of the National Honor Society and earned a football scholarship to Duke University.

Some faced academic adversity before they were able to harness the power of "and then some" and get back on track. Norman Borlaug, the man credited with feeding the world, failed his college entrance exam at the University of Minnesota. Chris Sullivan, founder and chairman of OSI Restaurant Partners Inc.—better known for such chains as Outback Steakhouse, Bonefish Grill, Cheeseburger in Paradise, and Blue Coral Seafood & Spirits—was on academic probation his sophomore year at the University of Kentucky. It was a real challenge for him to graduate, but he did. Like many, his probation was not for lack of trying, it was for lack of trying hard enough. George Shinn, entrepreneur and owner of the New Orleans Hornets, and the youngest person ever to be inducted into the Horatio Alger Association of Distinguished Americans, barely graduated from high school. After a few years of working in a textile mill he realized he needed more education, and worked as a janitor to pay his way through business school.

And while there were people for whom education was a family legacy, many more of our database defied the odds and became the first members of their families to attend college. The parents of Clarence Otis Jr., CEO of Darden Restaurants Inc., the largest casual dining company in the world, for example, both quit school by the fifth grade. But Otis received a bachelor's degree in economics and then went on to graduate from law school. Carol Bartz, CEO of Autodesk, had a father with only a second-grade education. She earned a bachelor's degree in computer science from the University of Wisconsin. Linda Alvarado, CEO of Alvarado Construction in Denver, Colorado, had a similar story. Her father had to quit school at age sixteen to help support the family after his father died. Although he would return a few years later to earn his high school diploma, that was the extent of his education. Alvarado graduated with a bachelor's degree in economics from Pomona College in Southern California.

Clearly, the members of our database didn't just complete their educations: As a group they *excelled* at academics despite significant strikes against them. The lack of money, the lack of a perfect academic record, and the lack of a family legacy of education didn't stop them from getting their education. None of the regular obstacles one can encounter in college—financial problems, flunking a class, poor instruction, bad health at critical junctures, stiff competition, you name it—stopped them, either. In short, not only did they matriculate, but they also graduated, and a sizable number continued their education past the undergraduate level. So important was education that they wouldn't let anything stand in their way.

We'd like to suggest that the power of "and then some" had something to do with our database members' perseverance in the face of adversity. Well schooled in the power of "and then some" because of their experiences in overcoming adversity, they were able to view what was adversity to others as a mere setback. They were well equipped to handle difficulties—in fact, so well equipped that once they found the power, they rarely fail at anything. And when they do fail, they are able to rebound.

A Formal Education Never Stops Giving

We hope that any student reading this book who is considering dropping out or trying to make a go of it without formal education has already banished those thoughts. We hope that any parent of a student who is considering dropping out or enrolling in the "school of hard knocks" will intervene immediately and convince them otherwise. Life experience and informal learning are crucial, but you can't make the most of any informal learning experience without the skills a formal education teaches you. Still not convinced? You don't have to take our word for it—let us show you what the members of our database of successful business professionals gained from a formal education.

For some, formal learning opened the door to the business world. More and more these days, a college diploma is required to gain entry-level qualifications for entry-level jobs. In short, you may not even be able to get your foot on the lowest rung of the corporate ladder without a degree. For others, gaining a diploma despite significant adversity was a huge accomplishment in itself, giving them confidence to rise to greater heights. For others, a formal education was a ticket out of humble beginnings, quite literally: College scholarships delivered them out of limited or downright awful circumstances and into vibrant new worlds with exponentially more opportunities. For still others, formal education got them out of stagnant situations; they knew they couldn't advance without a knowledge base that reflected both breadth and depth. And if money is what speaks to you, here are a few more statistics to consider: According to 2002 Census Bureau information, average yearly earnings for those eighteen and older were $18,826 for non–high school graduates, $27,280 for high school graduates, and $51,194 for those with bachelor's degrees. Education and earnings attainment may not be the measure of success for everyone, but they do indicate achievement, and the correlation between higher income and higher levels of education is undeniable. As for our database members, let's just say they're no strangers to financial success.

So let's review the benefits of a formal education. We've got job qualifications, increased confidence, a way out of humble beginnings, a way out of a stalled career or life situation, and a statistically better chance of greater earning power. It's a convincing lineup, but guess what? We still haven't told you what may be the most important advantage our business-savvy professionals gained from formal education.

The Thirst for Knowledge and Learning How to Learn

No matter what discipline our business-savvy professionals studied, every one of them gained an extremely valuable skill from formal learning, that of *learning how to learn*. Few people enter college with the intended purpose of learning how to learn, but where better than a formal learning environment? College is like an intellectual incubator—minds are nurtured until they gain the requirements for full maturity. A four-year undergraduate degree, no matter the major, teaches research skills; reading, writing, and speaking skills; critical thinking; time management; discipline; perseverance; and how to access information. It also exposes one to a broad range of topics, viewpoints, and people. These hallmarks of formal learning figure directly in later informal learning: Those who've been thoroughly trained in the tools of formal learning are more easily able to be self-motivated learners in later life, and they're well schooled in how to go about gaining knowledge. It's no surprise that those who excel at formal learning are better positioned to excel at informal learning. Remember that fully 80 percent of how people learn their jobs is through informal means. The business-savvy professionals in our database took their formal learning skills directly into the informal learning environment (i.e., the business world), where they often gained the bulk of the knowledge that enabled their success.

Lee Liu, for example, formally educated as an engineer, stated it this way: "It was not necessarily the knowledge I gained in college that was so valuable to me. It was the disciplines, the processes, the understanding of the importance of knowledge, and the creation of curiosity that made me a lifelong learner that were so important. I also learned to be a very practical person: As there is more knowledge available than is useful, I had to learn not to take on knowledge for knowledge's sake alone."

Business will always require one to learn new things and to adapt to new situations. The need to acquire new knowledge and skills will never cease, so the reality is that informal learning will be a lifelong endeavor. Why not equip yourself with the best possible preparation for being a lifelong learner, for learning how to learn? Business-savvy leaders require a nimble, well-informed mind, a knowledge base that reflects both breadth and depth, and the ability to be *enthusiastic* lifelong learners. Business will always have adversity, and it will always have unexpected opportunities. The business-savvy leader who is able to think on his or her feet and make informed decisions has a decided advantage over those who still find learning drudgery. Being able to think effectively and to learn is preparedness in itself, the preparedness not only to overcome obstacles but also to excel at every endeavor. If your formal education has taught you how to learn, your path to success will be all the smoother. If you've discovered a thirst for knowledge that you're eager to satisfy, you might just have some fun along the way, too.

Let's now meet a business leader who discovered his thirst for knowledge while still in his youth and who has used his incredible formal learning experiences to pave the way for a remarkable success trajectory, both in his business and his personal life.

Peter M. Dawkins

Some may recognize the name Peter Dawkins from his professional career in business as a retired vice chairman of Citigroup Private Bank. Others may recognize him from his winning college football's most coveted award, the Heisman Trophy. Still others may recognize him as a former candidate for the U.S. Senate or as a U.S. Army brigadier general. Remarkably, this is all the same man, just different arenas in which he has excelled.

Dawkins is originally from Royal Oak, Michigan, and started character building early in life by working summers on his grandmother's farm. His grandfather died when he was four, and as Dawkins grew he progressively played a bigger role in helping his grandmother. She eventually gave him five acres of his own that he plowed with a horse and grew cucumbers to sell to a local cannery. At a young age Dawkins learned to work dawn to dusk and enjoy it.

But at age eleven Dawkins contracted polio, which left him with a severe curvature of the spine. The typical treatment—a body cast—had a track record of unsatisfactory results. Dawkins's mother found an experimental treatment involving building up muscles on one side of the spine. It entailed years of rigorous two-hour-a-day physiotherapy workouts, but Dawkins was no stranger to hard physical labor. His robust physical work ethic and his commitment to the program precluded a lifelong disability.

When Dawkins entered high school he was a mere ninety-eight pounds, aptly carrying the nickname of "Squirt." But by the time he graduated he was a strapping 185 pounds and an All-League quarterback and captain of the baseball team. For many, sports are fantastic character and confidence builders, and that was certainly true for Dawkins.

Although he'd achieved in high school sports, college sports would be another uphill climb. He arrived at West Point as a quarterback, but in spring practice of his freshman year he was fired from the position and relegated to scrum running back. The setback inspired Dawkins to work even harder. "I was not a gifted athlete but an okay athlete and I worked my tail off," he said. He worked so hard, in fact, that he eventually won the Heisman while captaining the last undefeated Army football team. The achievements did not end on the football field, either. Dawkins was a much heralded Army hockey player and while attending school in England, one of the most written about rugby players.

Dawkins's physical and athletic achievements alone tell an incredible story, but what really intrigued us was Dawkins's twenty-one years of formal education. Here was a guy who had a rough academic start, but who learned from that adversity and made a remarkable turnaround. Dawkins went on to four years at the U.S. Military Academy at West Point, three years as a Rhodes Scholar at Oxford, and then earned a master's and a doctorate at Princeton University. We wanted to see what ignited that kind of thirst for knowledge and how Dawkins's education, both formal and informal, launched the competencies that led to his success.

Turning the Lightbulb On

With his many years in academia one would think that learning must have come easily to Dawkins, but the reality is quite the contrary. In junior high Dawkins struggled with his academics and like so many young people was unfocused and uninterested. This was partly his fault—"I was basically a truant, my hair was in a duck-tail, and I carried a switchblade," he said—and partly his school's. "The junior high I went to was a really weak school, submediocre," he said. "In seventh-grade English class we did not read and write English, but had English read to us." It wasn't until later that he recognized how poorly he was being educated and how lessons presented in such an uninspiring format stood no chance of capturing his interest. All the students were in the same boat. The school didn't have air-conditioning and his classroom was on the second floor. The kids would place their books on the windowsill and then "accidentally" push them out the window, a game just to waste class time. "The school definitely lacked discipline," he said. "I was bored and lacking direction."

Fortunately, his mother recognized that he was on a bad path and petitioned to get him transferred to Cranbrook, a nearby private school. It was no easy task, as the family could not afford the tuition and Dawkins had no basis for receiving a scholarship. His mother was very persistent, however, and in the end her efforts paid off. "My mom camped out at Cranbrook and would not go away," Dawkins said. "I believe they only gave me a scholarship to get rid of her."

At Cranbrook, Dawkins found the academics overwhelming. Totally unprepared, he found even routine assignments difficult, such as when he was asked to write a theme paper and had no clue what a theme paper was. He failed his first semester. The school elected to give him a second chance, and in his second semester he worked hard to catch up. Dawkins sees the time he spent at Cranbrook as a turning point, not only in his learning but also in his life. "That second semester I kind of got it, figured it out," he said. "The masters at Cranbrook were demanding, but they also wanted you to succeed. I was starting to get excited about learning. I became inquisitive and started reading on my own." Finally, inspired and intellectually stimulated, as well as held to high standards for the first time, Dawkins applied himself and became an honor student. It was just the first step on a path of tremendous academic achievement.

There were several contributing factors to the awakening of Dawkins's thirst for knowledge. The work character he gained in his long hours on the farm and overcoming a disability was important. He had a persistence that many his age did not, and an ability to see beyond a current adversity to the desired goal. He was no stranger to hard work and put in the long hours of study he needed to catch up and excel. He also had a parent who not only recognized a directional problem and its potential lifetime impact, but also found and campaigned for a change. The change in environment from his poorly performing school to Cranbook was a major trajectory adjustment for the better as well. It permanently removed him from a situation that was only bringing him down. Then there was the role of the teachers at Cranbrook. They required discipline, and they genuinely cared for him and wanted him to succeed.

But the main precipitating factor was the first semester's failure at Cranbrook. It was a significant adversity. He didn't want to fail again, especially after his mother had labored so tirelessly to get him admitted. He knew he was botching a second chance, a second chance he hadn't even earned. So he accepted the adversity of failure and determined then and there not to let it happen again. That second semester, Dawkins worked doubly hard. And in the act of learning, of really applying himself for the first time, something magical happened: He discovered the joy of learning. He became a self-starter, a student who sought out information on his own. He excelled both at the formal learning that Cranbrook offered and at the informal learning he conducted on his own time.

Dawkins is like many in our database: Once the lightbulb clicks on, they're overachievers in the realm of formal learning, as they are in so many arenas. It is the skills they learn in a formal setting, in learning how to learn, that lead them to become overachievers with informal learning as well. Our database was able to lean heavily on their informal learning abilities to learn new roles, grow businesses, and quickly adapt in rapidly changing business landscapes. And all along the way they understood that their knowledge base, which had allowed them to get to a particular level in business, was not adequate to get them to the next level. In other words, they recognized the continual need to learn more, and to acquire more knowledge, to advance. It's like that old saying: "What got you where you are today won't get you where you want to be tomorrow." The more you know, the more you realize how much you don't know. Those with a thirst for knowledge are indefatigable in filling their knowledge voids, and they enjoy doing so.

Learning How to Learn Applied

Cranbrook may have marked the turning point in Dawkins's life—the beginning of his thirst for knowledge—but his time at West Point was the most formative. At West Point he excelled all around. In addition to being captain of the football team he served as a brigade commander and class president, and he was a "star man," a distinction reserved for the top 5 percent of the class. "By the end of my time at West Point I definitely had the thirst for knowledge," Dawkins said. He described his West Point education this way: "Education develops skills in answering increasingly difficult and arduous questions. It teaches you how to find answers to very complicated questions. You also gain additional education such as time management and synthesizing, just to name a couple." He graduated with a degree in engineering.

The army has always been very aware of the power of knowledge, and it encourages kids to learn. Dawkins was accepted as a Rhodes Scholar and the army supported him by leaving him on active duty while he attended the University of Oxford in England. Rhodes scholarships have been issued annually since 1902 to approximately ninety scholars. They are granted on the basis of academics and strength of character. At Oxford Dawkins was struck by a different learning system. He attended lectures, met with a tutor, prepared a paper, and then presented the paper orally. For his first assignment he was given four books on the British Corn Laws and then left to his own devices. "I met with my tutor and asked what was I to write a paper on," he said. "He looked at me in utter disbelief and said, 'That is what *you* are to figure out.' West Point and Oxford were completely different learning methodologies, but when added together they meshed wonderfully." The four years at the military academy and three years at Oxford gave Dawkins a breadth of perspective, an ability to adapt to and flourish with different learning styles and in different environments. As you'll see, this intellectual plasticity would serve him well in the business world.

Oxford turned into a period of reflection, discovery, and important intellectual development for Dawkins. His studies were in the fields of philosophy, politics, and economics. He learned to read what people were saying, the exact meaning of their words, and what they were intending to say and communicate. "I learned the skill of being precise and careful with what I say," he said. "Words without precision create arguments—it's carelessness in language. The linguistics would prove to be extremely important to me. I learned to pay attention to what people are saying. What they really mean and what they say may not be the same. This was extremely important to me so I could be a guiding influence in leading, building coalitions, and minimizing conflicts throughout my careers."

The Turn to the Business World

After graduating from Oxford, Dawkins went on to a distinguished military career—a career spanning twenty-four years that required him and his family to move twenty-one times. He served in Vietnam and Korea and was decorated with the Distinguished Service Medal, the Legion of Merit with Oak Leaf Cluster, two Bronze Stars for valor, and three Vietnamese Gallantry Crosses. To satisfy his insatiable thirst for knowledge, Dawkins continued to add to his formal education, earning a master's of public administration (MPA) and doctor of philosophy (Ph.D.) from Princeton University. He would also complete a one-year term as a White House fellow. He accomplished all this before retiring from the army as a brigadier general at the age of forty-four.

Even with an ample knowledge base, the jump from the military to the private sector was not an easy one, as it had an urgent requirement called money. "When I left the military I had enough money to make it three months," Dawkins said. "When you work for the military you see it as a lifelong commitment and you do not plan for retirement." Through some friendships he started getting introduced to companies around Wall Street, though he admits that he "had no idea what a company would do with me." One of the companies he did not call on was Lehman Brothers. Friends had told him he did not want to work there, as Lehman's corporate culture was awful. He got a call from the CEO of Lehman, Lewis Glucksman, who had gotten wind that Dawkins had been bouncing around Wall Street job hunting. Glucksman asked Dawkins why he had not talked to Lehman and if he would be interested in interviewing with him. By this time Dawkins was within two weeks of being broke, so he reluctantly agreed to meet Glucksman for lunch. Dawkins candidly admitted he could not imagine going to work in the Lehman environment. Glucksman's response? Changing the environment was exactly why he wanted him. Dawkins was offered a job as partner and head of the public financing banking division. He accepted it the same day. Dawkins, who hadn't been able to imagine what the private sector might want to do with him, now had an idea.

He became the first partner at Lehman brought in from the outside. This raised some resentment among the existing partners, who believed Dawkins had not earned his stripes at Lehman. He was also placed over more than forty bankers—bright young Wall Street bankers, most of whom had liked their prior boss, who had been fired to make room for Dawkins. He describes the move as "a big leap of faith." He had to learn a new job on the spot, and as things turned out, it was a situation Dawkins found himself in repeatedly. "My entire career has been never knowing the job I was promoted to, and I was unqualified for each one," he said. "I became accustomed to new assignments and having no clue." Here's where the experience of being exposed to a plethora of learning styles and environments really paid off. Having received an exemplary formal education, having become well versed in learning how to learn, Dawkins aced the informal learning his private sector jobs required.

Remaining a firm believer in public service, Dawkins left Lehman Brothers after four years to run for the U.S. Senate for the state of New Jersey. With a history of being up to the challenge he ran against wealthy incumbent Frank Lautenberg, who had a seasoned and well-known campaign manager in James Carville. It turned into a tough fight and ultimately a narrow loss for Dawkins, precipitating his return to the private sector.

He joined the strategy consulting firm of Bain & Company as head of U.S. consulting practice. He was given a task that others saw as "mission impossible" at the time, providing key leadership through a very difficult and complicated transition from a founding leadership to a new generation of managing directors. Since then, Bain has reestablished itself as one of the preeminent firms in the consulting industry. After two years Dawkins was recruited away by Sandy Weill of the Travelers Group to run one of Travelers' subsidiaries, Primerica Financial Services, Inc.

The Atlanta-based financial services company had been in a tailspin. Dawkins was once again tasked with stabilizing and reinvigorating a company working its way through a difficult transformation. The company had a part-time sales staff of 100,000. For the next five years Dawkins, as the Primerica chairman and CEO, would provide the leadership that reestablished the company as the nation's largest seller of individual life insurance. Since then, Dawkins has held several senior positions in the world of Citigroup.

Formal Versus Informal Learning and the Ties to
Business Savvy

With Dawkins admittedly over his head in every new assignment or job, he clearly demonstrates that any amount of formal education is not enough and that informal learning has to take over. Initially important was getting the lightbulb of learning to come on, becoming curious and discovering the pleasures of learning, which happened at Cranbrook. Then West Point taught him to solve problems, to go linear and work the details. He learned to synthesize data into useful information, and between Cranbrook and West Point, he adopted the disciplines required to learn for a lifetime. Dawkins gained this with an engineering degree while others may obtain it through other areas of study, or informally. Oxford's totally different learning approach taught him to think with the big picture in mind, to think systems.

The needs for knowledge and for being able to learn hardly end once we get a degree; business will always require that we gain new knowledge. Those with a strong formal education background will be much more adept at the task of informal learning.

The great news is, when you've discovered your thirst for knowledge, learning becomes a welcome habit and is no longer difficult. When you've found a driving curiosity that you're passionate about, learning is pure pleasure. Business-savvy professionals thrive on knowledge because they *want* to, and because that's how they keep their businesses successful. They are as adept at gaining knowledge from a seminar or class as from the day-to-day experience of running a business.

Regardless of natural intellectual ability, struggles or successes with formal education, financial resources or lack thereof, a familial pattern of education or lack of one, something happened in the life of each of the database members to ignite that thirst for knowledge. They have active, restless minds that thrive on input. They have an insatiable thirst for knowledge, and they're enthusiastically indefatigable in working to quench it.

The Adversity Paradox Takeaways:
Get a Read on Your Thirst

- Our database of highly successful businesspeople shows a level of formal education higher than most, which attests to the importance of formal education in the creation of success.
- For most of these people, learning how to learn was developed during their formal educations. The lifelong learning habits they gained in a formal education environment enabled them to overachieve in their informal education.
- Your success is significantly impacted by the foundation of knowledge you have or will possess. If you haven't already found a thirst for knowledge, it's not too late. Enroll in a class, subscribe to a new journal, read as much as possible, travel whenever possible, and keenly observe successful people and emulate them. You never know when something will ignite your thirst for knowledge, but you do have to create optimal conditions for it. So be a sponge! Get out of your comfort zone and try something new or more challenging. Make learning an adventure!

9

Using the Adversity Paradox to Triumph Over Unexpected Trajectory Changes

Being business savvy, having a fully developed human capital, and performing well doesn't immunize one from having a career catastrophe. A sudden trajectory change can be caused by any number of adversities that are out of one's control, including technological advances that eliminate jobs, a natural disaster, illness, economic misfortunes, slipups, and unjust conspiratorial overthrow. The sudden loss of a career is disastrous for anyone, but the business savvy are able to rely on their human capital either to rebuild a career or reinvent themselves. Such success born of wholly unforeseen adversity is tantamount to overcoming the catastrophic.

It Can Happen to Anyone

Buzz Aldrin has one of the most recognized names in the world, and his early human capital accumulation landed him on the moon. He was an outstanding student and athlete in high school and was appointed by a New Jersey senator to West Point, where he graduated third in his class. He flew sixty-six combat missions in the Korean War and shot down two MIG–15s. Later, he attended the Ph.D. program at the Massachusetts Institute of Technology, where he developed and wrote a dissertation on orbital mechanics that would be used throughout the space program. Aldrin entered NASA in 1963, and the peak of his career was the July 20, 1969, historic Apollo XI moon walk, an event seen by the largest television audience in history. He was only thirty-nine at the time.

But only two years later, Aldrin left the space program, and his trajectory quickly went downward.

Aldrin loved space exploration, and the loss of a purpose and his passion devastated him. His life was soon complicated by depression and alcoholism. It wasn't until 1978 that he was able to establish sobriety, and eventually he went on to write four books. "The difficult part of my life was not going to the moon," he said, "it was what I faced when I returned."

Aldrin is hardly the only high-profile figure who was able to reestablish a success trajectory after a devastating loss. Steve Jobs was fired from Apple in 1985. After gathering himself and reevaluating his purpose and passion he went on to found the computer company NeXT. In 1996, Apple purchased NeXT for $400 million and Jobs returned to Apple, reviving the company with such breakthrough products as the iPod and iPhone.

Lee Iacocca had a thirty-four-year career at Ford marked by a steady stream of successes and innovation, including both the Mark III and the Mustang. As Ford's president, he was fired just shy of his fifty-fourth birthday. His trajectory change was caused by having too much success and overshadowing a man whom many described as a dictator, Henry Ford II. It was devastating to Iacocca at the time, but he went on to reestablish himself and resurrect Chrysler from the grave.

Both of these executives were blindsided by a trajectory change. They may have been very business savvy, perhaps even exceptionally so, and they may have had contingency or disaster recovery plans in place, but nothing could prepare them for the sudden separation from companies to which they'd devoted their lives. Even though the business savvy are recognized for their ability to see around corners, no one can predict the future with 100 percent certainty. The good news is that most adversities or career catastrophes leave a person's human capital substantially intact. Trajectories may be shaken by the unpredictable but they can be reestablished—sometimes with far superior results.

My Coauthor's Story

I met my coauthor, Bob Jennings, in 1990, a couple of years after I arrived in Des Moines to take my position as a vice president with The Principal. He had recently moved from the Los Angeles area with his wife and two sons. This appeared to be the last of many moves, nine in ten years, as he climbed the corporate ladder, the third generation in a small, 400-employee and sixty-year-old company. We met playing tennis, and had entered a tennis tournament to compete in doubles. Our first match was on a Friday evening, and Bob showed up late, past the default time. He claimed to have been handling a very important and complicated overseas conference call. He was thirty-one years old at the time and I was having a little trouble buying it. Only when researching this book did I learn that his call was with a French bridge designer and contractors from Canada and Australia. They were building a $140 million elevated roadway project on the island of Oahu, Hawaii.

In the years that followed we continued to play tennis tournaments and he was never late again, lending credibility to his story. He continued to climb the corporate ladder of his construction equipment supply company, eventually becoming president, which was no surprise to me. Bob was clearly passionate about his business and a real go-getter. What's more, it appeared to be his destiny: The company was an old-line company, manufacturing-based, started during the Depression by Bob's grandfather. Over its first sixty years or so it had grown to about 400 employees, surely with some ups and downs. Then in a relatively short period of time, a renaissance occurred. There was tremendous sales and profit growth and the company expanded to 1,200 employees worldwide. Bob mentioned, with pride, that historically his company had never had a losing year.

When it came to business there was a fearlessness in Bob, and definitely a hunger. He was constantly peppering me with questions about how my company did various things, like employee recruitment, sales hiring, training, sales motivation, compensation, personnel appraising, handling of expatriates, foreign currency exchange, and succession planning. I remember thinking that I wasn't the only person he was asking for information.

At Principal we were in the process of jump-starting our own fledgling international expansion, difficult even with all our resources. Meanwhile Bob had a brutal travel schedule; in one particular year he did seventeen all-night flights. It wasn't a vagabond style of travel, either, and his family was extremely important to him. Typical trips were all-night flights to Buenos Aires or Santiago and then straight to the office for a long day. He would work Saturdays in Kuala Lumpur and the next day travel to East Malaysia to meet with Muslim contractors who worked on Sundays. Domestically, he would be on the first flight out in the morning, and when he returned, the last flight in. He adhered to a self-prescribed no-alcohol policy while on the road, and dinners were normally something picked up at a local grocery store and taken back to the hotel room. Over that period of rapid growth he did five round-the-world trips, most in coach class. To me, it sounded like blue-collar work being done in a white shirt.

But Bob loved what he was doing, and his work character was clearly paying off. He was published in trade magazines, something no one in his company had previously accomplished, and he held patents for different kinds of construction equipment, something that was quite foreign to me. He had started his climb at an entry-level sales position, risen through the ranks, and had a higher education, more experience, and greater achievements than any of his predecessors. To me, he was not the quintessential small-family-company guy.

Then, just when I was really starting to believe that everything he touched turned to gold, 2004 came and Bob suddenly found himself without his company and his job. Gone, out on his own. A career catastrophe. What appeared to be a protected business environment apparently had more land mines than I could have ever imagined. Having then known Bob for fourteen years I knew his departure was not an issue of his compromising his values and had absolutely nothing to do with results. It was one of those unavoidable and totally unforeseen career catastrophes that blindsides a person and leaves him reeling—especially in this case, as Bob was in love with his work and completely focused on growing a business, so much so he had no plan B. I knew it was ugly when I gave him the book *We Got Fired,* by Harvey Mackay, and he said he'd received the same book from three other people.

Why This Story Is Important for The Adversity Paradox

When Bob and I started writing this book, we assembled a think tank to provide feedback and the occasional gut check. The members served as an outstanding mirror. We included the CFO of a major media conglomerate, a college professor and consultant who had at one time worked on the Apollo space program, and a retired Baptist minister who was raised in a broken home in the projects of Chicago. Through the early stages of book development they loved our premise, concepts, framework, and stories but recognized our failure to address the all-so-common midcareer trajectory change—which is clearly its own special brand of adversity. They raised the need to address career catastrophes, especially unforeseen ones. Without Bob's change in trajectory we would have never written this book.

Telling Bob's story also provided me with a great opportunity. My weeks were filled with the demands of being the CEO of a Fortune 500 company, which left much of our book research and legwork up to Bob. He conducted many of the interviews, and he invariably left them excited and enthusiastic and newly inspired by the great stories he'd heard. Interviewing Bob was my opportunity to jump in and get a taste of the frontline action. Not until after the interview did I realize, in all these years of our friendship, that most of what I'd seen of my coauthor was his veneer, made up of humility coupled with the camouflage of self-deprecating humor. There was much about Bob I didn't know, and all the puzzle pieces began to fall into place when I heard the full story of his midlife adversity.

A Third-Generation Company

Bob's grandfather, W. A. Jennings, started a company that designs and manufactures forms for concrete construction. W. A. Jennings earned eighteen patents revolutionizing concrete forming in his day. He got his start supplying contractors in 1934, usually for the construction of schools, churches, and various structures that were all or partially concrete. The company grew through emphasis on civil markets with the construction of bridges, stadiums, dams, power plants, and water-treatment facilities.

Like a lot of business-savvy entrepreneurs, W.A. exhibited the key trait of being able to overcome adversity. He started a successful business during the Great Depression, a time when it was much more common for companies to be going out of business. The underlying human capital components were also apparent in him. He had a tremendous work character, and the patents demonstrate his purpose with passion and his thirst for knowledge. When W.A. died in 1980, the company was placed in the hands of two of his sons, in hopes that future generations could enjoy and add to the fruits of his labor.

Construction was in Bob's blood. He had no problem finding his purpose, as it was instilled in him and adopted at a very young age. Family vacations always included side trips to tour construction projects. The projects, never small, included bridges, football stadiums, basketball arenas, and nuclear power plants; they were, at the time, some of the largest projects in the world.

Throughout his early years, the company was involved in such construction projects as the Seattle Kingdome, Houston Astrodome, and Busch Stadium, just to mention a few. Bob's purpose, the family business, came early. His passion, to build the largest concrete structures in the world, would soon follow.

Working hard was his family's tradition, so early on he developed a strong work character. Allowances were not given but earned. He started full-time summer work before the ninth grade as a draftsman for the company, drawing concrete outlines and equipment. He had to drop his favorite sport of baseball and thus he learned early on about sacrifices. Money was never really an issue, as he was always earning. He didn't make a lot per hour, but he worked a lot of hours.

At the age of eighteen he left the confines of the drafting room, joined the iron workers' union, and worked in the manufacturing plant the next couple of summers. At one point the iron workers went on strike, but Bob kept working. "There probably should have been some sort of moral dilemma as I was crossing a picket line where I saw people I'd befriended in my summer work," he said. "On the other side of the gate I had my family business. But all I was concerned about at the time was the greenbacks. Cash was still king to me."

For continued experience he later joined the carpenters' union and worked for a local construction contractor. "I worked for one contractor but several job-site superintendents," he said. "When we would finish a job they always thanked me and said they looked forward to getting me back on future jobs. I never did forget their appreciation, and I decided this was something I wanted to carry on should anyone ever work for me someday." The last summer before his college graduation he returned to the family company, providing field services on large construction projects. They included bridges in Canada and Michigan, the Metrodome in Minneapolis (home of the Vikings), and the elevated Metrorail in Miami. While following a purpose, a passion was beginning to be aroused.

Purpose and passion, work character, and at least some cursory introspection were in place, but his values behavior and thirst for knowledge were much different issues. In fact, they may have been nonexistent through high school and college, a lack he admits was detrimental. "I was conducting introspection but not learning the right things," he said. "It must have been like a house of mirrors at a carnival. From an early age I was constantly getting into fights and would occasionally come home with a black eye. In the fifth grade I was playing sandlot football with older kids when I got into a fight and broke my arm while I was being thrown around like a rag doll. In the ninth grade I thought I had found some success in sinking the winning basket in overtime of a basketball game, but I'd talked trash to the opponents the entire game and got beaten up afterward. These kinds of scuffles were fairly common. There were flaws in my values behavior that would cause me to get into fights for years to come."

His honesty and integrity also suffered in those years. In high school he was fired from his first formal, punch-the-time-clock job outside the family company—he was a janitor for a Montgomery Ward store—for unethical behavior. Meanwhile the juvenile delinquent days continued. Even a sound beating by the police after an altercation at a hotel, while he was a senior in high school, didn't knock sense into him. In fact, if it hadn't been for work, the outcome for Bob might've been thoroughly disastrous.

"I'm thankful for the work character and purpose that was provided by my parents, which gave me some leverage to get away from self-destructive behavior and a downward spiral," he said.

As for his thirst for knowledge, it's no surprise that at the time, Bob had little enthusiasm for formal education. Informal education, such as reading books or being involved in extracurricular activities other than sports, was also not part of his program. In his early days at Iowa State University he just squeaked by, but eventually friends demonstrated to him what it took in the way of studying, and smart roommates helped pull him through.

So, at this stage in Bob's life, an assessment of his overall individual human capital looked something like this:

Introspection   A house of mirrors and little or no real introspection.

Values Behavior   He sat very low on the values chain. Probably stage 2.

Work Character   Excellent work ethic and enough perseverance to pull him through undergraduate school.

Purpose and Passion   A well-defined purpose and a growing passion.

Thirst for Knowledge   Absolutely none.

Finding the Missing Parts

After college Bob married his fiancée, Janet, who had recently graduated from the University of Iowa with a computer science degree. She had grown up in a town in rural Nebraska, was the daughter of a family doctor, and had excelled academically. This kind of marriage, one having some pretty radical differences, can have a profound effect on people. The introduction of a new mirror can either be disastrous or harmonious. Fortunately for Bob, it was the latter.

Engineers were a hot commodity when he graduated from Iowa State in 1981, and though his GPA was about average, his résumé was attractive, given his work experience. This provided him a couple of offers from great companies having outstanding management-training programs, such as Texas Instruments and the Brunswick Corporation, the company best known for billiards and bowling equipment. He believed the Brunswick offer would be exciting and that purpose and passion might follow. At the same time, his passion for the business he grew up in was still strong, and as it happened, the family company was looking at taking its top-performing North American products into foreign markets. Bob couldn't resist the lure of going overseas, and he knew he'd regret it if he didn't follow his passion, so the new couple decided to follow Bob's purpose and passion and make whatever sacrifices were required to do so. He accepted a sales position in Santiago for a salary about half of that of his engineering offers, and within weeks of being married Bob and Janet relocated to Chile. As for Janet, computer science was also a hot degree at the time and the couple assumed she'd quickly find work.

Their financial situation soon proved bleak. Bob's hope was in making sales commissions, but the challenges were formidable. No one from the company had ever set foot in Chile, and given its size, the company had little experience in foreign markets. Chile wasn't exactly a hospitable market, either. It had an emerging third-world economy and was under a relatively new dictatorship. It had a wealth of natural resources and high copper prices and was export driven. "We had some savings," Bob said, "but for the first time in my life I was carrying debt in the way of my wife's school loans." And Janet couldn't get through the bureaucracy to obtain a work permit in Chile. After six months, she found work at the United Nations Latin American headquarters, which was based in Santiago and exempt from work-permit requirements. So much for using her computer science degree.

The couple had no budget for furniture, so they borrowed a mattress, a propane cook stove, and a black-and-white TV and bought a couple of folding chairs. There was a two-year waiting list to get a phone, but they later found out that it didn't matter, as their apartment building had no access to phone lines.

Living under the military dictatorship of Augusto Pinochet was a real eye-opener for them. "Every Sunday, a tank convoy would drive by our apartment, we assumed to show the masses who was in charge," Bob said. "Neither of us grew up around guns, so the occasional roadblock and vehicle search while a soldier stood ten yards away with his machine gun pointing at you, bullet clip in, was plenty unnerving."

Another hardship the couple faced was a feeling of isolation. Although Bob worked diligently on his Spanish, it was very weak. There were no English TV stations, radio stations, papers, or publications, and the dictatorship censored news and information within the country. They were unable to receive the Voice of America but could sometimes dial in the British Broadcasting Corporation by radio.

Then, not long after they arrived, the price of copper fell and the fragile Chilean economy fell with it. As the economy slowed, available construction opportunities dried up. "This left a lot of idle time to fill, and we were without the usual outlets that we grew up with such as sports, movies, TV, dinners out, and finding trouble," Bob said. "I was fortunate that my wife was an avid reader and had stuffed her suitcase with a multitude of books. She was a real trooper and never complained despite the circumstances. We also found a couple of street news vendors who had connections with workers who cleaned airplanes that had flown in from the United States. They supplied us, most weeks, with tattered *Time* and *Newsweek* magazines, which we'd read cover to cover." The reading began as a means to fill idle time, but soon began to create a real thirst for knowledge. The more Bob read, the more he realized that there was much he didn't know, and that he might not have the skills he needed to be successful.

One thing he did have was a 300-pound sample set of his company's equipment. He toted it around to contractors and gave demonstrations. "I felt like the door-to-door Kirby vacuum salesman of the day." To haul his demo around he borrowed a minivan from newfound Chilean business acquaintances. It had a 60cc engine and ten-inch wheels—smaller wheels and engine than the Honda 125 dirt bike he'd owned in college.

Despite Chile's economic downturn he had some success with sales, which included part of a hydroelectric dam about four hours south of Santiago. The customer was a joint venture of Chilean and Spanish contractors. For the type of equipment he was selling, instruction and training were often required. He jumped on the opportunity to conduct the field service, which entailed working on-site and living in the construction camp for four weeks. Given world communication systems at the time, there was no good way to phone for help or advice. "If you had problems, either personal or business, you figured them out," he said.

With available opportunities dwindling in Chile, Bob cast his sales net over a wider area, making trips to Buenos Aires, Argentina, and Lima, Peru. During his first trip to Buenos Aires there was a military coup that brought General Leopoldo Galtieri into power. "They don't exactly advertise those things ahead of time," Bob said with a grin. Argentina's economy was struggling at the time with hyperinflation, and Galtieri would soon lead Argentina into the Falkland Islands and a war with the United Kingdom.

Several trips to Lima resulted in the successful sale of another hydroelectric project high in the Andes located on the Urubamba River, a tributary to the Amazon, near the famous Machu Picchu Inca ruins. He agreed to service the project and traveled to a remote construction site and camp high in the Andes. This entailed flying into the town of Cuzco and then boarding a train for a scheduled six-hour trip. The train had wooden seats and was filled with mostly indigenous people, along with some of their live poultry. "For me, it was truly something I had only seen in the movies, at best," Bob said. During the trip, the train was stopped by a landslide, and Bob was stranded overnight—in pitch black in the middle of nowhere.

While staying at the construction camp he inquired into ways to return to Cuzco upon completion of his work via a tourist train that serviced Machu Picchu. The return trip was comfortable and uneventful, taking only four hours, although not long after that, the Shining Path guerrillas, who were increasingly expanding their areas of control in Peru, blew up the train, killing a number of tourists.

The Downside of Life Might Be the Upside

"My wife and I had graduated from college, hot degrees in hand, ready to make our mark on the world," Bob said. "Our decisions placed us in an underdeveloped country with a repressive government, taking money out of pocket to get by, no phone, and sleeping on a mattress on the floor of an apartment. But what looked and felt like the downside of life was anything but. For the most part, all my wife and I had was each other. This would galvanize a relationship that might have not survived otherwise."

His values were still shaky but changing. Living in an underdeveloped country will make you question many things. For starters, the world might not revolve around you. He was starting to recognize that he needed to bolster his human capital. "In hindsight, I see that I possessed the purpose and passion that created the needed fortitude and perseverance," he said. "My passion and purpose could have been shaken but it was actually bolstered. I was taking new technology to third-world countries and building some of the largest and coolest construction projects in the world. But my biggest shortcoming was my lack of a thirst for knowledge, and it was becoming painfully apparent for the first time in my life. I realized there was so much I needed to know." The lightbulb was coming on.

So, at this stage in life I would evaluate his individual human capital as follows:

Introspection   Lots of soul-searching is going on. He has at least one mirror in a spouse, and is starting to look for added mirrors for some triangulation. He is starting to harness the power of "and then some."

Values Behavior   Starting to develop. He has a spouse with strong values and is gaining experiences that are impacting faith, honesty, and integrity. He makes a move up from stage 2, "what's in it for me," on the hierarchy of moral development.

Work Character   Starting to build on his already sound physical work ethic and on his cognitive work ethic. Leadership skills would come later.

Purpose and Passion   Continues to carry him.

Thirst for Knowledge   His curiosity is awakened.

After a year, Bob and his wife departed Chile, and his company would not return for a number of years, until the economy improved. But when it did, their operation, employing more than a hundred nationals of the country, would become one of the company's shining stars. The country has done well with democracy in place and boasts the largest emerging middle class in all of Latin America.

Moving On

The next step on Bob's career path was a transfer to Dallas, Texas, where he took an entry-level sales position with his family's company. This was a position he'd thought below him when he graduated from college, but he needed a job and realized beggars couldn't be choosers. His wife quickly found work with Tandy Corporation, which was doing well at the time with its Radio Shack stores and the desktop computer, the hot-selling TRS-80. Their earnings soon outpaced expenses, for the first time in their lives.

Although the Dallas area seemed like Shangri-La to them, Bob's sales territory and its history were another story. In the years just preceding, it had been one of the worst-producing sales territories for the company, partially because it was a home base for the company's biggest competitor. No surprise that the territory was available!

He was given an office, a phone, a file cabinet with a handful of old customer files, and a K-car and told to go to work. His boss, the district manager, was released not long after he arrived and not replaced. "My first six months I sold nothing," Bob said. "The economy was a little rough, but most of all, customers were content with their current suppliers and my company's reputation in the area had taken some hits with performance issues. I hated cold calls, over the phone or in person, but committed to it and got over my call reluctance. I burned up the highways and put over 33,000 miles a year on my car. When I would lose a project I always followed up by talking to the contractor in person and seeing what I needed to do better next time." His potential customers saw him more than they saw their current suppliers, and it paid off. Customers also became a great mirror, providing instant feedback; and in the construction industry it was rarely sugarcoated.

Over a three-year period Bob became the number-two sales representative in the company. Not a huge deal, as there were only forty at the time, but unprecedented because he was a twenty-six-year-old kid. He had gone from not winning any sales to almost never losing a sale. Momentum was contagious. He thrived on it and so did his team members. The district went from upside down to setting company sales records that would not be broken for many years, most of that time without a manager.

Continued Human Capital Growth

Just as the South American experience had done, the direct sales stint continued to impact Bob's human capital growth. Relationships with customers started to drive his moral development. "I remember the first couple of times I fudged the truth," he said, "telling customers their shipments would be on time when I knew darn well they wouldn't, or I failed to mention some potential hidden costs. Those customers were mad forever, slow to pay, and reluctant to do business with me again. For those with whom I was straight up and honest, they oftentimes got mad, but they got over it and sometimes later even thanked me for being forthright. In other cases I saw how finding the best exchange in value for my customers would provide for sustained sales growth." Honesty, integrity, and trust had started to come into play as prioritized values, and he continued to move up the hierarchy of human development.

His rapidly developing work character had started to pay off also. Long trips with a lot of the driving done after normal business hours between Dallas, Austin, San Antonio, Corpus Christi, and parts of west Texas gave him the reputation among customers as the guy who wanted their work the most. He had started to hone some skills as well: time management, communication skills, meeting and sales call preparation, listening, and accountability. He recalls in particular his development of the ability to have empathy: "There was nothing more important, when trying to gain a meeting of the minds with a customer or teammate, than being able to put myself in his shoes. My efforts at selling, when it was all about me and my products, were a disaster, and only when it became about my customers and truly providing the best exchange of value possible did I get results."

So, at this stage in life, we could evaluate Bob's individual human capital development like this:

Introspection Teammates and customers were becoming mirrors, making introspection easier and more accurate. This was a very formative time in his life. The harnessing of the power of "and then some" was starting to show.

Values Behavior   There was a tremendous amount of development here, as a result of work as a frontline sales representative. Honesty, integrity, and trust were becoming priorities. A new concern for and understanding of how others felt and thought demonstrated a climb up the hierarchy of human development—a tough climb from being self-centered, at stage 2, just a few years before. He was beginning to see stage 5, where he could understand and be socially responsible.

Work Character   Real skills are being developed: presentation skills, organization, and other critical tools for being a business professional.

Purpose and Passion   Continues strong.

Thirst for Knowledge   Increasing development, primarily with the awareness of the need to know more.

Filling the Big Knowledge Void

As Bob became more skilled at pursuing his passion, his knowledge voids increasingly bugged him. The more he learned, the more he understood how little he knew. At the time, he'd pushed his commission-based income up from nothing to what anyone would consider great money, especially for his age, but he made the difficult decision to forgo the big money and go back to school to get his MBA at Southern Methodist University.

Graduate school at SMU was a fantastic experience, as he was engaged in learning like no other time. Courses were nearly 100 percent case-study based, a departure from the lectures and detailed problem-solving tasks of his engineering training. His grades reflected his commitment and effort.

With his MBA, Bob also achieved a level of education never achieved in his family. In fact, higher education was frowned upon. He had repeatedly heard growing up and in his first years at the business that "master's degrees are overeducation." I'm sure the business contributions he was able to make after his MBA changed everyone's minds for good.

During this time he also learned a lot about his company. Managers provided him full access to their financial history so when the occasional school paper or project came along he had a company he knew well and was passionate about to use for material. One assignment was an accounting paper involving the study of historic financials, looking for good and bad trending. "I was ecstatic to get an A on the paper," he said, "but surprised when the professor included a note asking me to schedule a meeting with him. A bit scary, as in my prior educational experiences the only time I was summoned to see the teacher, the circumstances weren't good. But the point of the meeting was a total surprise. My paper contained all the usual strategies an MBA student would include, like becoming the low-cost producer, creating teamwork, and increasing employee training, but I had missed the most important trend, which could only be seen by looking at the big picture. My company had ever so slowly been shrinking in size, which was masked by the high inflation of the times. It caught me off guard, as I had just come from overwhelming success in a sales territory and had been part of a team that had been successful setting company records in both growth and profitability.

"I'm thankful for my professor's mentoring. He recognized my passion for the business and that I would probably be going to work there after graduation, and he extended a helping hand."

Moving On to Managing People

After graduation, Bob, his wife, and a new son moved to San Francisco, where he would be taking on his first real role of managing people. The Dallas team experience had been great, as he saw a group of young people come together and develop their own corporate culture of trust, openness, and optimism, which delivered results the company had never seen before. His MBA education provided him with myriad additional tools that would be helpful, but nothing would prepare him for what he would need to learn on his own.

His new assignment had him managing people, offices, and facilities in California, Nevada, and Arizona that had notoriously underperformed. He was like many young managers in believing he could make anyone successful, and his first challenge turned out to be his best friend from junior high, high school, and college. It was something of a coincidence that his friend had landed with the company in California, but not totally. Companies can be notorious for employing friends.

After working closely with his friend for six months, Bob found himself in the miserable position of having to fire him. "He was failing when I arrived and when he left," Bob said. "Firing him was one of the most painful things I've ever done. He was a good person but wasn't equipped to handle the demands and the skills the position required. Regrettably, we have not talked for years, and if I had it to do all over again, I would find other options."

The personal pain was acute, but the hard decision did produce operating improvements. By now Bob had increased his business savvy, so he put the painful experience to work: He became an expert in recruiting, candidate screening, employee selection, compensation, and employee training. When asked to reflect, he says, "Like anybody, I'm averse to pain, and unsuccessful employees are particularly painful. You have to do everything possible to improve the odds."

He would take his new expertise continually to new heights as he climbed the corporate ladder, helping to create unprecedented company growth. Over the first couple of years the area would double its sales volume. His friend was not the only casualty, as he proceeded to upgrade a number of positions as he raised the bar on expectations. On the brighter side, the high-performing employees loved it. They could finally spread their wings and not be weighed down by competency issues of surrounding team members. As he doubled the size of the operation he moved his family, then with two sons, to the Los Angales area to open a new office and distribution facility. His team continued the growth pattern, and he was eventually promoted to VP and moved back to headquarters in Des Moines, Iowa.

"There were so many things that I learned," Bob said. "The setback of firing a best friend hurt, but at the same time I learned a lot about myself and others, and how and when to give feedback. Then the very first person I had intended to fire not long after I arrived on the West Coast became a top performer and was promoted several times in the years to follow, eventually becoming a well-respected VP. The very first time I gave him positive feedback, which was hard for me at the time, I did it in writing. He was located in Fresno, California, and the next time I visited him I saw my letter posted on his office wall. I thought it was a joke, but he pointed to it and said it was the first pat on the back he'd ever received from the company. What's amazing is how many years it took me to employ something I had seen years earlier.

"Most important for the company, I learned how to grow the

business and what was important—things like recruiting and employee selection, the importance of employee training, the setting of performance metrics, professional and teachable sales methods, and the need to have savvy people and scalable processes."

So, at this stage in life we see a pattern has developed:

Introspection He has an increased sensitivity to mirrors. The power of "and then some" has been harnessed.

Values Behavior In leading teams for the first time, he was starting to see the importance of leading by example and the need to live by values to do so.

Work Character Skills to lead were being added that would lead the organization to unprecedented growth.

Purpose and Passion Continues strong.

Thirst for Knowledge The thirst has been substantially developed.

Expanding Opportunities

It was at this point in his life that I first met my coauthor. He was then a VP and in charge of sales and service for the western half of the United States. His role would continue to expand, next taking on sales and service for the United States, then worldwide sales and service, and eventually all operations including manufacturing. With expansion he took the family company's forty-person sales force to 120. He had the human capital and subsequent business savvy to do so. He and his teams started operations in Buenos Aires, Lima, Taipei, Kuala Lumpur, Mexico City, and Manila.

There were certainly some bumps along the road. Construction is a high-risk and cyclical business. There was a construction recession in the late 1990s that meant some layoffs—painful but fortunately not to the degree of prior construction recessions. The fact is my coauthor had established a trajectory that he would not only continue with, but would also expand to his company and its many its employees.

Over this time he was able to follow his purpose while fulfilling his passion to be involved in some of the largest projects in the world. This included a $2 billion toll road in Bangkok consisting of thirty-five miles of elevated six-lane roadway, the Confederation Bridge, a bridge across seven miles of ocean connecting Prince Edward Island with mainland New Brunswick, and a host of large mass-transit projects and the traditional complement of stadiums and arenas.

I asked Bob what he thought his biggest contribution to the company and industry was.

"It was probably the development of a new product line where I had to use all my industry experience, engineering skills, market and competitive awareness, management skills, and team building. This was something that was unique, had lots of innovation, took the company into new markets, and in time would help redouble the size of the company." He's also the holder of one of the company's key patents. The product has had a lasting, indelible impact on the industry and is increasingly used on projects throughout the world.

And then, seemingly at the apex of his success, disaster struck.

Catastrophe

After years with his company and after a deep emotional investment in the family business, Bob was separated from his company without warning.

"My separation was most likely caused by an accumulation of differences in values and contrasting passions," Bob said. "Each one taken by itself was almost nothing, but stacked on each other over time led to the irreconcilable." As I saw it, the light was beginning to shine very brightly on Bob, and his leadership was being confused with attempted control and dominance of the company. "I never cared for or worried about control of the company," he said. "That was not my mission. I was much more interested in growing a business and a group of people to be the greatest they could be."

Some business misfortunes just happen.

Postcatastrophe Analysis

Using the power of "and then some," the most important reflection to conduct after a catastrophe is not necessarily on the catastrophe itself but on the taking of an inventory of your human capital. The purpose is getting on with life and re-creating yourself where needed. A catastrophe is only the elimination of a current means—it's never the loss of human capital.

In the case of my coauthor, and as in many in similar situations, Bob agreed not to compete with his company after the separation. He was suddenly bereft of his purpose, and he had signed away his passion. But if there was an immediate silver lining to be found, it was that knowing conclusively what he would not do got him looking elsewhere more quickly. Postseparation, his human capital inventory looked like this:

Introspection   This would be a new challenge, as many of the mirrors such as employees, customers, and results were gone overnight.

Values Behavior   Intact, and perhaps with even stronger convictions.

Work Character   He retained all the skills he had developed over the years. Some of those skills might be industry specific but many could be applied elsewhere.

Purpose and Passion   Gone.

Thirst for Knowledge   Some of the prior-knowledge foundation, having been profession specific, and field expertise gained became useless, but by having acquired the drive for lifelong learning, he was set to learn new skills.

Applying the Power of "And Then Some"

Bob recognized that he needed to take everything he had in his human capital inventory and apply it to finding a new passion or a purpose that held enough promise that he could potentially become passionate about it. I saw him dabble with venture capital, work with some private equity firms, and do consulting, everything from top-level strategy development all the way down to the factory floor with lean manufacturing. I even saw him go back and get some formal education and become a black belt in Six Sigma. With some things I could see the fire in his belly start to return. The more he put his catastrophe behind him, the bigger the fire could burn for doing something else.

Then, after attending a Horatio Alger inductee ceremony in Washington, D.C., with our wives and hearing yet another group of inspiring stories, he approached me with the idea for this book. Our intent from the beginning was to understand what allows those who have come from humble beginnings or who have undergone terrible adversity to overcome their difficulties, while others cannot. Bob rightly suspected that the book would not only challenge his thirst for knowledge but also would be a project we both could become passionate about. We were agreed from the beginning that one of our primary motivations in writing the book was to share what we knew and had learned so others could improve their lives.

Throughout the writing process he made various comments which can best be summed up with this final human capital inventory:

Introspection   "I would have never thought that having to replace the majority of my mirrors would be so difficult. A lot of sorting and sifting has been required to gain triangulation. But a change in mirrors can be very good, and turned out to be so in my case. With new mirrors you invariably find some of your older mirrors weren't reflecting accurately."

Values Behavior   "In doing your own thing, there is no pressure to compromise your values."

Work Character   "It was so important to me all my life and I have been so fortunate to be able to use it to regain trajectory."

Purpose and Passion   "Before my separation from the family company I had no idea how such a large void in my life could occur. My passion had clouded my vision. Who would have thought I could be too passionate about anything? After such a large adversity, new passions will always be much more grounded."

Thirst for Knowledge   "My lifelong learning desires were gained when I was in my midtwenties. Getting a chance to better satisfy those curiosities and create new ones has been fantastic, and my thirst for knowledge was instrumental in helping me overcome my midlife trajectory change."

With a solid human capital foundation and the business savvy he gained from triumphing over a midcareer setback, Bob gained a whole new life, one at least as challenging and as much fun as his prior life, if not more so.

The Adversity Paradox Takeaways:
Your Own Human Capital Development

* Maybe you haven't faced a midlife trajectory change, but the chances for being blindsided are always there. Take an inventory of your own human capital development and the history of your success trajectory. What adversities have had an impact on you? How did they impact you? Did they cause you to do some human capital building?
* If you missed an opportunity for human capital building, figure out right now how you can benefit from the experience: It's never too late. Hindsight is always twenty-twenty; what did you learn from the adversity? How can you use what you learned to positively impact wherever you are right now in your career trajectory?
* If you evaluated yourself as strong in any of the human capital components, how have they helped you overcome adversities? If you're weak in any, what concrete steps can you take to strengthen them?

Epilogue
Practicing the Paradox

So often, the most powerful catalyst for change lies in the place we'd least expect or want to find it—in adverse circumstances. Failure has a way of making us take stock of our careers and our lives—our progress toward dreams and goals, our strengths and weaknesses, our motivation, and our daily work habits—in a way that success does not. It can also force us to take quick, decisive action without benefit of the usual safety nets, which can often reveal inner resources and abilities we wouldn't have otherwise known we possessed. At the very least, overcoming difficult circumstances always causes growth and the development of your human capital. No matter what happens, nothing can take that hard-won human capital away from you. So if you find yourself in the midst of adversity, try looking at it from a different angle: Hardship always hurts, but you may be in the perfect position to make a major leap forward on your journey toward success and personal fulfillment.

If you're currently struggling with some sort of adversity, you're far from alone. Some of the most successful people in business today have built their accomplishments upon the very experiences that seem to promise failure. When you can overcome adversity and bring the positive lessons you learned to bear on your business and in your personal life, you've set yourself up for extraordinary success. If you're one of the few who has yet to experience significant adversity, you can still learn from and be inspired by those whose lives exemplify the adversity paradox. Like the business leaders you've met in these pages, we've been through all manner of misfortunes in our careers, and undoubtedly we'll face them again. But we can assure you that when we applied the power of "and then some" to overcoming obstacles and learning from the experience, we not only recovered from setbacks but emerged smarter and savvier, and even more committed to remaining on an upward success trajectory. You can do this, too.

Adversity, large or small, will always happen. When difficult circumstances arrive, banish thoughts of negativity, discouragement, or surrender. Take responsibility for any role you played in creating the setback, but don't get caught up in blaming yourself or engaging in the kind of self-pity that precludes action. Your job now is to implement a straight-A approach: Accept adversity, analyze it, approach it with the right attitude, and tackle the entire process of self-improvement with a generous dose of "and then some." *Accept* whatever hardship has come your way. Tempting as it may be to try to avoid responsibility or negative consequences, you won't get anywhere by denying the facts. *Analyze* the situation so you can determine how to prevent the same mistake and so you can learn everything possible. *Approach* the challenge with the right *attitude,* a positive frame of mind, and with the intent to make adversity your friend. Harness the power of *"and then some"* with each of these steps, and you're well on your way to uncommon success.

If you can accept the wisdom the adversity paradox offers, you can count on emerging from difficult situations with the kind of business savvy you can't get from any course, seminar, or training program. So get on the unconventional path to business success right now. Find opportunity in obstacles. Regard setbacks as a chance to start anew with more focused intentions. Befriend adversity, and let the adversity paradox lead you into a realm of business and personal success you never suspected was possible.

APPENDIX

Name	Success in
Aldrin, Buzz	Space exploration
Allbritton, Joseph	Banking
Allumbaugh, Allen	Restaurants
Alvarado, Linda	Construction
Anderson, Walter	Publishing
Andreas, Dwayne	Food processing
Angelou, Maya	Literature and education
Anschutz, Philip	Oil
Antonini, Joseph	Retail
Argyros, George	Real estate
Barrett, Barbara	Government and aviation
Barrett, Colleen	Commercial airline
Barrett, Craig	Microprocessing
Bartz, Carol	Software
Beall, Donald	Aerospace
Bedell, Tom	Fishing equipment
Behring, Kenneth	Real estate and non-profit
Blavatnik, Leonard	Oil and gas

Name	Success in
Boeckmann, Herbert II	Auto dealerships
Borlaug, Norman	Agriculture
Bossidy, Lawrence	Technology
Brin, Sergey	Internet
Brokaw, Tom	Television news
Brown, Dorothy	Medicine
Brown, Jack	Retail grocery
Buffett, Warren	Investing
Buntrock, Dean	Waste management
Cain, Herman	Restaurants
Cantrell, Wesley	Telecom equipment
Cantu, Carlos	Business services
Carson, Ben	Medicine
Cathy, Truett	Restaurants
Chambers, Raymond	Investing
Christopher, Doris	In-home sales
Ciocca, Arthur	Food and wine
Clark, Mary Higgins	Writing
Colloton, John	Hospital administration
Copley, Helen	Publishing
Cortopassi, Dean	Food processing
Courtelis, Alec	Real estate
Cousins, Thomas	Real estate
Craig, Jenny	Weight management
Craig, Sid	Weight management
Crandall, Robert	Commercial airlines
Crow, Trammell	Real estate
Cuban, Mark	Pro basketball
Cundy, Thomas	Insurance
D'Alessandro, Dominic	Financial services
Dasburg, John	Air cargo
Davidson, Dick	Rail transportation
Dawkins, Pete	Financial services
Dedman, Robert	Private clubs
Dejoria, John Paul	Hair care
Dempsey, Jerry	Glass
DeVos, Richard	In-home sales

Name	Success in
Dobbs, Lou	Television news
Donlon, William	Utilities
Doré, Bill	Marine construction
Doti, James	Education
Dougherty, Michael	Banking
Dudley, Joe Sr.	Hair care
Dunham, Archie	Oil
Durham, Charles	Engineering
Egan, Michael	Auto rental
Ergen, Charles	Media and entertainment
Fertel, Ruth	Restaurants
Fiorina, Carly	Technology
Fox, Sam	Investing
Frankfort, Lew	Apparel
Gary, Willie	Law
Gates, Bill	Software
Gibson, Duane	Religion
Giles, Terry	Law
Gill, Jack	Venture capital
Graziadio, George Jr.	Banking
Greehey, Bill	Natural gas
Griswell, J. Barry	Financial services
Grundhofer, John	Banking
Hagadone, John	Media
Hall, Craig	Real estate
Halliday, Ebby	Real estate
Harken, Tom	Public speaking and writing
Harp, Lore	Software
Haslam, Jim	Travel centers
Hendricks, Rick	Auto racing
Holt, Dennis	Media
Huizenga, Wayne	Diversified business
Huntsman, Jon	Petrochemical
Hutchings, James	Fabricating
Iacocca, Lee	Automobile
Ivester, Douglas	Beverage
Jacobson, Allen	Technology

Name	Success in
Jannetta, Peter	Medicine
Jennings, Bob	Construction technology
Jobs, Steven	Technology
Johnson, Thomas	Television news
Jones, Clay	Aerospace
Joseph Robert Jr.	Real estate
Kelly, Dee	Law
Kelly, Patrick	Medical equipment
Kemp, John	Non-profit
Keough, Donald	Beverage
Kesler, Delores	Temporary staffing
Keys, James	Convenience stores
Kimsey, James	Internet
Klein, Melvyn	Investing
Knight, Philip	Athletic appeal
Knowlton, Richard	Food processing
Kroll, Alex	Advertising
Lansing, Sheri	Filmmaking
Lee, James	Investment banking
Lenfest, Gerry	Cable television
Lerner, Alfred	Real estate
Liu, Lee	Utilities
Mack, John	Investment banking
Mackay, Harvey	Manufacturing and writing
Marcus, Bernard	Home improvement
Mars, Forrest Jr.	Food and candy
McCain, Warren	Drugstores
McCaw, Craig	Wireless
McKenna, Andrew	Restaurants
McPherson, Frank	Energy
Milgard, Gary	Glass
Moffett, James	Minerals
Moore, Gordon	Microprocessing
Moran, Jim	Auto dealerships
Mozilo, Angelo	Mortgage banking
Neubauer, Joseph	Business services
Nicholson, James	Real estate

Name	Success in
Nidetch, Jean	Weight management
Novelly, Paul	Oil
Omidyar, Pierre	Internet
Ornelas, Louise Herrington	Cable television
Otis, Clarence Jr.	Restaurants
Overby, Charles	Media
Page, Larry	Internet
Pappajohn, John	Venture capital
Patterson, James	Restaurants
Pattison, Jim	Auto dealerships
Pearson, Ron	Retail grocery
Perot, Ross	Technology
Pichler, Joseph	Retail grocery
Pickens, Boone	Energy and investing
Pohlad, Carl	Banking
Poling, Harold	Automobile
Pomerantz, Marvin	Packaging
Portman, John Jr.	Architecture
Qubein, Nido	Education
Radia, Suku	Banking
Rapoport, Bernard	Insurance
Resnik, Frank	Tobacco
Rinker, Harry	Real estate
Ritchie, David	Auction
Roach, John	Electronics
Roderick, David	Steel
Rosenberg, Richard	Banking
Rouse, James	Real estate
Rubenstein, David	Private equity
Russell, Herman	Construction
Sander, John	Financial exchange
Schott, Stephan	Home building
Schuller, Robert	Religion
Schultz, Howard	Coffee shops
Schwartz, Robert	Insurance
Scott, Ray	Fishing tackle stores
Scott, Walter	Construction

Name	Success in
Siebert, Muriel	Brokerage
Simon, Robert	Manufacturing
Sims, Naomi	Cosmetics
Sinegal, James	Membership buying
Sokol, David	Energy
Soros, George	Investment
Steward, David	Technology
Sullivan, Chris	Restaurants
Taylor, Jack	Auto rental
Terlato, Anthony	Wine
Thomas, Clarence	Law
Tillman, Robert	Home improvement
Tippie, Henry	Investment
Trout, Monroe	Health care
Turner, Fred	Restaurants
Turner, Jim	Bottling
Turner, Ted	Cable television and broadcasting
Ventres, Romeo	Food industry
Vernon, Lillian	Catalog sales
von Furstenberg, Diane	On-air sales
Waitt, Ted	Technology
Walgreen, Charles III	Drugstores
Waranch, Ronald	Real estate
Washington, Dennis	Construction
Welch, Jack	Diversified business
Welters, Anthony	Health care
Westcott, Carl	Auto dealerships
Willingham, Ron	Training
Wilson, David	Auto dealerships
Winfrey, Oprah	Entertainment
Wolk, Sidney	Insurance
Wright, Michael	Grocery retail
Yang, Jerry	Internet
Yanney, Michael	Investing

NOTES

1. What Is Business Savvy, Anyway?

The format of the dictionary definitions of "business savvy" and "the adversity paradox" is based upon Merriam-Webster's online dictionary: www.merriam-webster.com.

The *Forbes* issue we're referring to is a special issue, "The Richest People in the World," March 24, 2008.

Basic biographical information on John Pappajohn is drawn from his Horatio Alger biography, which can be found at http://www.horatioalger .com/member_info.cfm?memberid=PAP95 and an article by Michael Lovell, "John Pappajohn: Venture Capitalist and Philanthropist," *The Des Moines Register,* October 27, 2003.

Biographical information on every Horatio Alger member can also be found in the Horatio Alger publication *Only in America: Opportunity Still Knocks,* which is released annually. John Pappajohn is featured in the 1995 issue.

The bulk of material in chapter 1 is based upon three interviews with Pappajohn in March 2008 and two interviews with Doug Stickney in March 2008.

The article containing Howard Gardner's thinking on synthesizing is "The HBR List: Breakthrough Ideas for 2006," *Harvard Business Review,* February 1, 2006.

The material on systems and linear thinking and communication is from Peter Senge, *The Fifth Discipline: The Art and Practice of the Learning Organization* (New York, NY: Currency Doubleday, 1990).

2. The Individual Human Capital of the Business Savvy

The definition of human capital comes from Gary S. Becker, "Human Capital," *The Concise Encyclopedia of Economics*. A copy of the article can be found at: http://www.econlib.org/library/Enc/HumanCapital .html.

All information on J. Barry Griswell is from his interviews with Bob Jennings. Please also see the 2003 edition of *Only in America*.

The *Forbes* global 2000 list can be found at http://www.forbes.com/ 2008/04/02/worlds-largest-companies-biz-2000global08-cxsd0402global land.htm.

3. The Power of "And Then Some"

Duane Gibson was interviewed March 9, 2007; Larry Jorn was interviewed January 26, 2008; Gene Postma was interviewed January 25, 2008; and Suku Radia was interviewed March 28, 2007. Information on Sheila Holzworth is from an internal Principal publication: "Breaking Down Barriers" (*Comment*, The Principal Financial Group, February 1989), 5–9, and conversations with the authors in 2007 and 2008.

There is a profusion of material on the role of optimism and the power of positive thinking in attaining success and personal fulfillment, but we are particularly indebted to the work of Martin Seligman, especially his *Learned Optimism: How to Change Your Mind and Your Life* (New York: Knopf, 1990). The terms "learned optimism" and "learned helplessness" and the information on how optimists tend to do better in myriad ways than their pessimistic counterparts come from this book. Two other books that influenced our writings were Norman Vincent Peale's *The Power of Positive Thinking* (New York: Prentice-Hall, 1952) and Maxwell Maltz's *Psycho-Cybernetics* (New York: Prentice-Hall, 1960).

There are a variety of sources on the Millennials. One good place to start is Morley Safer's segment on CBS News, "The 'Millennials' Are Coming," available online at http://www.cbsnews.com/stories/2007/11/08/60minutes/ main3475200.shtml.

4. Just Add Introspection

We have only scratched the surface of Ben Carson's remarkable story. For more, see his Horatio Alger biography at http://www.horatioalger.com/member_info.cfm?memberid=car94, this short essay in his own words at http://www.npr.org/templates/story/story.php?storyId=4950531, from which our material comes, or the 1994 issue of *Only in America*.

The material on Peter Dawkins is from his Horatio Alger biography, which can be found at http://www.horatioalger.com/member_info.cfm?memberid=DAW06 and his Web site, www.petedawkins.com, and a personal interview conducted September 5, 2007. Additional information can be found in the 2006 edition of *Only in America*.

The source of information on Harvey Mackay can be found in his book, *Swim with the Sharks Without Being Eaten Alive: Outsell, Outmanage, Outmotivate, and Outnegotiate Your Competition,* (New York: Harper-Business Essentials, 1988), and from conversations the authors had with him throughout 2007 and 2008. Additional information can be found in the 2004 edition of *Only in America*.

Material on Lee Liu comes from a personal interview on March 8, 2007. Additional information can be found in the 1999 edition of *Only in America*.

Information on Doris Christopher and the early days of the Pampered Chef are from *The Pampered Chef: The Story of One of America's Most Beloved Companies* (New York: Random House, 2005), and a personal interview with her, April 9, 2007. Additional information can be found in the 2006 edition of *Only in America*.

Warren Buffett's comment is from the foreword to Christopher's book, *The Pampered Chef*.

The quotation is from Ron Willingham, *Integrity Selling: How to Succeed in Selling in the Competitive Years Ahead* (New York: Broadway Books: 1987).

5. What Does Behavior Have to Do with Values?

The quote from Plato can be found at http://www.brainyquote.com/quotes/authors/p/plato.html.

Kohlberg's theory on moral development can be found in the first volume on his essays on moral development: Lawrence Kohlberg, *The Philosophy of Moral Development*, vol. 1. (San Francisco: Harper and Row, 1981).

The source of the quotation from Howard Gardner is in Bronwyn

Fryer, "The Ethical Mind: A Conversation with Psychologist Howard Gardner," *Harvard Business Review* 85, no. 3 (March 2007), pp. 51–56.

6. Sorry, but There's No Substitute for Hard Work

Both authors have heard Ron Willingham's story in person and have paraphrased it here. A version of it can also be found in his *Integrity Selling: How to Succeed in Selling in the Competitive Years Ahead* (New York: Broadway Books, 1987). The authors had numerous conversations with Willingham throughout 2007 and 2008.

The *Fast Company* interview can be found at http://www.fastcompany .com/magazine/74/fasttalk.html?page=0%2C2.

The second quote from Robert Joss can be found at http://aaroncole .com/examples/gsbmba/.

The Gallup survey on employee recognition is cited in Marcus Buckingham and Curt Coffman, *First, Break All the Rules: What the World's Greatest Managers Do Differently* (New York: Simon and Schuster, 1999).

The NORC study on job satisfaction (which also includes data on workers' general happiness) can be found at http://www.norc.org/NR/ rdonlyres/2874B40B-7C50-4F67-A6B2-26BD3B06EA04/0/JobSatis factionintheUnitedStates.pdf.

The quote from Harvey Mackay is found in his *Swim with the Sharks Without Being Eaten Alive*.

A copy of Albert Gray's essay can be found at http://www.the intellectualviewpoint.com/reading/thecommondenominatorofsuccess-al bertengray.pdf.

7. Purpose and Passion—You Really Can Take the Work Out of Work

The full text of Dr. Martin Luther King Jr.'s speech can be found at http://stanford.edu/group/King/publications/papers/vol3/561203.000-Facing_the_Challenge_of_a_New_Age,_annual_address_at_the_first_ annual_Institute_on_Nonviolence_and_Social_Change.htm.

Material on Norman Borlaug is taken from Leon Hesser, *The Man Who Fed the World: Nobel Peace Prize Laureate Norman Borlaug and His Battle to End World Hunger* (Dallas: Durban House Publishing Company, 2006).

Kenneth Quinn's quote on Norman Borlaug was given directly to the authors on March 11, 2008.

All material on Clay Jones is from a personal interview, February 28, 2008.

The article citing that people aged 18–38 change jobs on average ten times can be found at http://careerplanning.about.com/b/2006/07/28/how-often-do-people-change-careers.htm.

The results of the CNNMoney poll can be found at http://money.cnn.com/2007/01/15/magazines/fortune/job_survey.fortune/index.htm?postversion=2007011709.

The U.S. Bureau of Labor Statistics survey can be found at http://www.bls.gov/news.release/nlsoy.nr0.htm or at http://www.bls.gov/nls/nlsy79r19.pdf.

Material on Walter Scott is from the public record and a personal interview, March 4, 2008. Additional information can be found in the 1997 edition of *Only in America*.

8. The Transformative Power of a Lifelong Thirst for Knowledge

Basic biographical material on Peter Dawkins is from his Horatio Alger biography, at http://www.horatioalger.com/member_info.cfm?memberid=DAW06 and his Web site, www.peterdawkins.com. The remaining material comes from a personal interview, September 5, 2007.

Our database of business-savvy leaders comprised 200 people, 80 percent of whom are Horatio Alger members. Individuals whose education records could not be validated through public sources were not included.

9. Using the Adversity Paradox to Triumph Over Unexpected Trajectory Changes

The material on Buzz Aldrin comes from his Horatio Alger biography, which can be found at http://www.horatioalger.com/member_info.cfm?memberid=ald05. Additional information can be found in the 2005 edition of *Only in America*.

All information on Bob Jennings is based upon interviews with Barry Griswell.

ACKNOWLEDGMENTS

The Adversity Paradox was not written in a vacuum. We will be the first to admit we needed and received lots of help.

At the top of the list is the Horatio Alger Association of Distinguished Americans. Our learning firsthand about a group of individuals who have lived the adversity paradox triggered our desire to write this book. Listening to their stories and seeing a number of these remarkable people inducted into the association truly inspired us.

Many special thanks go to our think tank members, whose input and feedback were invaluable. When we organized the group we had a good idea of our needs, but these people went above and beyond. They read countless versions of various chapters, diplomatically corrected us when we were off on tangents, and displayed a singular dedication to seeing us write a good book. Duane Gibson, a retired minister and a man who knows the adversity paradox well, having come from humble beginnings himself, was our spiritual leader. Dr. Roy Park, retired professor and business consultant, made sure we were in tune with academia and always broadened our perspective. Suku Radia, an immigrant to the United States who overcame great difficulties to become a highly successful community and business leader, gave us great insights time and time again.

We'd also like to extend our thanks to two successful businessmen and authors we're honored to call friends. Ron Willingham and Harvey Mackay are seasoned veterans, and they provided outstanding coaching throughout the writing of *The Adversity Paradox*.

We are particularly indebted to all those who agreed to and patiently endured our interviews for this book. Our questions often were not easy for a group notable for their humility as much as their success, and we appreciate that they moved past their comfort zones to offer us candid personal stories. We are also grateful to the many other individuals who, upon hearing about the project, shared their own stories of overcoming adversity.

Very special thanks go to our spouses, Michele Griswell and Janet Jennings. They have not only been our lifelong partners but also great mirrors who scoured the manuscript numerous times, and were often our most helpful critics.

Most important, we must acknowledge some very special mentors: our parents, families, and friends who, all along the way, saw our potential and helped us find faith in ourselves.

When we started writing we thought we had all the elements to write a successful book: talented think tank members, mentoring from two highly respected and successful businessmen-turned-authors, a long list of potential interviews, and our experiences and success in business. But there was something we misjudged—our ability to write. Our editor, Catherine Knepper, has been with us almost from the beginning and she has been fantastic. She is a true professional and was a terrific team member on the project.

Finally, many thanks go to our agent, Doris Michaels, of the Doris S. Michaels Literary Agency, and to Phil Revzin, senior editor with St. Martin's Press, both of who saw potential in us and put *The Adversity Paradox* on the bookshelves.